TIME AND TIDE
sea of faith beyond the millennium

sf

BOOKS

ISBN 1 903816 00 9

Typography by Graham Whiteman

Write to:
John Hunt Publishing Ltd
46A West Street
Alresford
Hampshire SO24 9AU
UK

Cover picture: *Northern Landscape with Dark Trees, 2000* painted by David Blackburn (private collection). Reproduced by kind permission of the artist and Hart Gallery (London and Nottingham).

A CIP catalogue record for this book is available from the British Library.

Printed in Guernsey, Channel Islands

Visit our web sites at: johnhunt-publishing.com
www.sofn.org.uk

CONTENTS

CONTRIBUTORS

Don Cupitt is a fellow of Emmanuel College, Cambridge

Anne Ashworth is a poet and lives in Blackpool

Stephen Mitchell is Vicar of Barrow-upon-Soar in Leicestershire. He is currently Chairman of the Sea of Faith Steering Committee

Karen Armstrong, a former Catholic nun, is a best-selling author and broadcaster on feminism and the history of religions. She is author of *The History of God* and the recently published book on fundamentalism, *The Battle for God*

Dan Cohn-Sherbok is a rabbi and Professor of Judaism at the University of Wales. He is author or editor of over 60 books, which include studies of Judaism and other faiths

Paul Davies is Visiting Professor in the Physics Department at Imperial College, London, but lives mainly in Australia. He is author of *The Mind of God,* and in 1996 he won the Templeton prize for Progress in Religion

Michael Elliott is Education and Development Worker for the Sea of Faith Network. He is author of *Freedom, Justice and Christian Counter-culture*

Patti Whaley is Deputy Secretary-General of Amnesty International

Richard Holloway was until recently Bishop of Edinburgh and Primus of the Episcopal Church in Scotland. He is the author of many critiques of traditional religion, including *Dancing on the Edge* and *Godless Morality*

Graham Shaw, author of *God in our Hands,* is an Anglican Quaker

Lloyd Geering is Emeritus Professor of Religious Studies at Victoria University (N.Z.) and a member of the New Zealand Sea of Faith. His latest book is *The World to Come*

Philip Knight attained his PhD in theology at the University of Durham and works as a teacher of Religious Education

Robert Ashby, Director of the British Humanist Association, was keynote speaker at the 1998 Sea of Faith Conference at Sheffield University

Pamela Donohue was a poet and lived in Sheffield

EDITORS

Teresa Wallace, editor of *This is My Story,* is Convenor of the Sea of Faith's Publications Sub-Committee

Peter Fisher, editor of the Sea of Faith newsletter, *Portholes,* lives in Sheffield

Helen Fisher is Local Groups Co-ordinator for Sea of Faith

Michael Elliott is Education and Development Worker for the Sea of Faith Network

David Hart is Senior Lecturer in Religious Studies at the University of Derby

Dedicated to the memory of Pamela Donohue,
who organised our annual conferences
for our first twelve years
with warmth, calmness and efficiency

Sea of Faith has been "exploring and promoting religious faith as a human creation" for some 12 years now, and many people have ebbed and flowed through the Network in their search for a life which has meaning and purpose. The turn of the millennium seemed a propitious time to invite some critical comment about how the Network is regarded in today's religious climate and how it might develop its ideas for the future – and that is the task that the writers of this collection of essays have addressed.

In his introduction, Stephen Mitchell traces the development of the Network, commenting that while members agree in their understanding of faith as a human creation, "non-realist" is only one of the several labels members choose to apply to themselves. Others include "radical Christian" and "religious humanist" – standpoints which are reflected by our contributors.

The starting point that all members have in common is the recognition of the new intellectual and cultural environment that has been developing apace over the last two decades. The globalisation that Lloyd Geering talks about is not only about economics; Richard Holloway believes that it has also had an inevitably eroding effect on the way in which traditions are held. Patti Whaley, in talking of the widespread loss of belief in metaphysical foundations and absolute values, describes the resulting confusion: do we revive, create a new form, or abandon religion altogether? Whilst parting company with Don Cupitt's denial of "a stable mind-independent world out there", Paul Davies applauds him in leading us into new understandings of the role of language and culture in shaping our world view. The resultant marginalisation of Christianity has meant that the churches have reacted by adopting a "siege mentality" – a point made by Michael Elliott in connection with the Church of England and by Richard Holloway in relation to the conservative leadership of the Roman Catholic Church in Scotland.

In examining Sea of Faith's concept of religious faith as a human creation, Robert Ashby is fascinated to have found a place where he, as a humanist, is able to share this understanding. Richard Holloway asserts that there is no escaping our own creative role: the stories all come from us, and whether there is any "beyondness" to them is the great unanswerable question. While Lloyd Geering believes that all of our concepts, including our concept of God, have been humanly created, Graham Shaw is more equivocal. He accepts that God is a human creation, but maintains that our creation has a life of its own and warns against exaggerating the extent of human responsibility in this creation.

In this new era, when belief in metaphysics and absolutes seems to be rapidly dissolving, the question of what we understand by the words "truth" and "true" is a challenging one, and most of our contributors touch on this, explicitly or implicitly. Paul Davies, in explaining why we should take science seriously as a path to truth, exemplifies Newton's inverse law of gravity as "simply true" – a fact which is independent of the cultural milieu from which it emerged. Philip Knight, following the pragmatism of the philosopher Richard Rorty, holds that the word "true" has a practical rather than representational significance – it is what helps. Graham Shaw, who looks askance at the Church of England's attitude to truth, finds that his way to truth is a process of spiritual learning, an existential approach in some ways analogous to that of Patti Whaley.

Our writers offer a range of suggestions for the future of Sea of Faith, with Dan Cohn Sherbok suggesting that the emergence in America of two non-supernaturalist Jewish movements should offer inspiration to members of Sea of Faith. Patti Whaley sees the Network sharing ideas with the human rights movement, working with them in defence of religious freedom. She suggests that our task is not to argue whether God is true, but to explore ways in which the religious demand helps us to achieve a better life – a point taken by Karen Armstrong, who believes that only by practising the compassion which is taught by all the major traditions will we find a glimpse of the Sacredness which gives meaning to our lives. For Michael Elliott, dialogical education is the way forward: open-minded exploration grounded in human experience. A sombre Lloyd Geering believes that the Network should focus on the future of the planet – for him, the chief religious issue.

Don Cupitt, whose thinking, writing and encouragement have helped so much in nurturing the development of the Network, has the hope that Sea of Faith may be seen as "the new Socrates", possessing no ideology of its own, but forever questioning. He quotes Nietzsche in the prologue – "Don't follow me, follow yourselves" – which exactly mirrors his relationship to the Network. We need to be free to create a religious society "that doesn't inhibit its own members, but actively encourages each member to find and to develop his or her own voice".

The ideas in this collection of essays, coming as they do both from outside and within the Network, are a refreshing stimulant for Sea of Faith – and we believe our readers will be equally invigorated by them.

Teresa Wallace, Peter Fisher, Helen Fisher,
Michael Elliott, David Hart

THE FREEDOM OF THE SEA

Anne Ashworth

The Freedom of the Sea!
Has it been conferred on you?
No ceremony, no certificate.
It's not like that.

The ancient seas of faith purported freedom.
Once, it was said, a man walked on water.
Many have pretended hard,
Stood on dry land
Insisting it was wet.

Brave ones struck out, swam far.
Admire them.
But who's free in the water?
At length, at sea, however oiled their bodies
They founder in the unnatural element.

Are mariners free? – masters of navigation
Who know the ropes, the lore, the shipping lines?
Their well-drilled crews, their trusting passengers?
For all the charts, engines and instruments
Shipwrecks still happen.

Some say, to gain a Freedom
You need a shipwreck first.

Losing your boat, your books, you navigate
By the wide sky only.
Growing your wings, you rise,
You skim the surface,
Frolic in breakers, float awhile in calm,
Soar with gulls on thermals.

You love the sea? All right.
No need to lose touch.
Just don't depend on it.
Pause now and then on islands if you like.

Fly on. Find fresh companions.
Dance on outrageous winds.
Dare new horizons.
Offer yourself the Freedom of the Sea.

INTRODUCTION

Stephen Mitchell

In the year that the BBC broadcast *The Sea of Faith*, Margaret Thatcher had been in office for five years. A coking plant in Orgreave was the scene of violent clashes between picketing miners and riot police. An IRA bomb devastated the Grand Hotel in Brighton. David Jenkins was consecrated Bishop of Durham and York Minster was struck by a bolt of lightning. Boy George became the nation's pop idol. Michael Jackson broke all record sales with *Thriller* and Jayne Torvill and Christopher Dean's interpretation of Ravel's *Bolero* won them an Olympic Gold medal in Sarajevo.

It was the Orwellian year at last. Mikhail Gorbachev had not yet come to power in the Soviet Union. The Berlin Wall had not yet become the gateway to the West and the wreck of the *Titanic* had still to be located.

The Sea of Faith Network was a child of the eighties. The first Sea of Faith conference was convened in 1988 and a year later the Network was formed with the statement of intent "to explore and promote religious faith as a human creation". Following Don Cupitt's lead in the television series and the book *The Sea of Faith*, its members sought to work out the implications, both for the church and themselves, of the declaration that faith was "wholly of this world, wholly human and wholly our own responsibility". The agenda was radical and Christian, the membership mainly elderly and male.

But stripping religious faith of supernaturalism and affirming the view that faith, like art, springs from the heart of human creativity, plunges religious belief into the politics and fashions of changing culture. It's no longer 1984 and Sea of Faith is coming to terms with its baptism in late twentieth-century culture.

The first survey of Sea of Faith's mailing list, carried out in 1991, suggested that nearly half of the 250 members were aged between 51 and 65. Seventeen per cent were over 65 and another 17 per cent were in the 16–35 age range. Seventy per cent were regular churchgoers, and half were Anglicans.

Some of these were priests who had made long and sometimes painful journeys in faith. One such radical parson was John Hodgkinson. He described *A Radical Parson's Progress* in the first edition of the *Sea of Faith* magazine, a journey made by many people of his generation, lay and ordained:

Born in 1927, I grew up within the church, and with an assurance of God's presence and power. The step to ordination seemed a natural progression from all that I had known, and it was linked with a desire to serve, the prospect of adventure, and sheer wonder at the complexity ... of the universe.

Acknowledging growing doubts about a God "out there" with the publication of John Robinson's *Honest to God* in the 1960s, and wrestling with questions of Christ's divinity reinforced by *The Myth of God Incarnate* in the 1970s, he was pushed to the limits.

It became difficult to continue as a parish priest, to preach the orthodox faith and yet retain my integrity. The temptation was to cut loose from the pain, to fall back on infallible revelation and to push the intellect in the background, or to leave active ministry. To battle on was to accept a very real cross. Deep down I knew that the Christian faith worked, for the experience of suffering accepted, and death and resurrection, were at the heart of human experience. The fellowship of love within the church, the celebration of birth, marriage, death and holy communion, all continued to be effectual means of grace.

Discovering Jung and reading *The Sea of Faith* enabled John to pass through the pain barrier.

One year later, in an isolated villa on an Aegean island I read *The Sea of Faith* a second time. Now I was able to take the final step, and to accept God as the sum of my values, and to pursue a religion that didn't depend upon a supernatural being, or a revealed set of infallible truths. As with all conversions, the sense of relief was enormous ... Once I had passed through the pain barrier and relinquished the old, I found [my faith] was given back to me with a new vitality ... an inexhaustible treasure house had been opened up to me.

Hodgkinson's pain echoes the "eternal note of sadness" that Sophocles heard on the Aegean and to which Matthew Arnold refers in his poem *Dover Beach*. For Arnold, writing in 1867, the Sea of Faith was once "at the full". Now with a "melancholy, long, withdrawing roar" the sea was retreating. The world was changing. Christianity was being marginalised.

Pain and sadness can be the experience of those undergoing conversion and the Network provided a safe haven for many on their journeys of faith. But as Arnold's lover sees the world lying before him "so various, so beautiful, so new", and as Hodgkinson found new vitality in his old faith, so the hope of those attending the first Sea of Faith conference was that the tide could turn again and faith could be renewed and become once more an inexhaustible treasure house. Their concerns, expressed on the application forms, were to do with the reinterpretation of Christianity, its practice in prayer and worship, its expression in ethics and social action and its promotion in the face of fundamentalism. Was a non-supernaturalist interpretation possible? Did faith need a new story? Could it be practised and preached with integrity? Upon what was its spirituality and ethics to be based?

By no means all of those joining the Network and attending the annual conferences were Anglican priests or even church members, but two events in the early 1990s caught the public attention and cast Sea of Faith in an Anglican mould. On Easter Day 1992, the BBC was accused of providing a platform for heresy. A. N. Wilson made an announcement to his *Sunday Telegraph* readers:

> Tonight on *Heart of the Matter* Joan Bakewell will be talking to three brave clergypersons who do not believe in the resurrection of Jesus, or indeed in any of the miraculous elements of Christianity. There exists, apparently, something called the Sea of Faith Network, a group of 200 clergy who share the belief that "God is a creation of the human mind".

The following year there was an even bigger controversy. Brian Appleyard, writing in *The Independent*, recognised the consequences of taking the debate beyond doubts about the resurrection to the very existence of God.

> It is at this point the Rev. Anthony Freeman, formerly of St Mary's Church, Staplefield, West Sussex, enters the big picture. He has been sacked for writing a book – *God in Us* – in which he appeared to say he did not believe in God. As far as he was concerned this did not disqualify him from being a Church of England priest; as far as his bishop and part of his congregation were concerned, it did.

> In thus becoming the first priest this century to be dismissed for his theological views, the mild, hesitant, amiable and symbolically named Freeman finds himself uncomfortably projected into the historical role of the great dissident, an English village version of Giordano Bruno or

Martin Luther. It all feels slightly absurd and so, unsurprisingly, the affair has been treated as a rather pastoral comedy or as yet further evidence of the irremediable decline into fatuous liberalism of the Church of England.

And yet, as Appleyard points out, Freeman was saying nothing that had not already been said by Cupitt in *The Sea of Faith* in asserting that religion is "wholly of this world, wholly human and wholly our own responsibility". Appleyard asks:

> Leaving the rights or wrongs of the theology aside, this raises two distinct questions: does the Church of England need a "real" God? And, since Cupitt and Freeman are clearly determined to preserve a central role and identity for their deity, does Western society need any kind of God?

Convinced that society does need its communal commitments he concludes:

> Whatever you might think of this faith, at least it shows an awareness of history and tradition that is completely lacking from all other ideologies around which the West has tried to organise itself. It convinces its adherents that the culture as it is, and has been, is worth sustaining rather than mindlessly rejecting.

By 1995 the Network had grown to over 750 and attracted a more varied and less masculine membership. In a survey of *Sea of Faith* magazine readers, more than two out of three had a continuing church connection. Nonetheless, while 33 per cent said they were closely associated with the Church of England, almost as many, 31 per cent, had no religious affiliation. One in three subscribers was a teacher or lecturer while 16 per cent were clergy or those in training for the ministry.

The most common labels members were prepared to use of themselves and their faith were "non-realist" (nearly 30 per cent) "radical Christian", "Christian humanist", "religious humanist" and "post-Christian". The labels were important in distinguishing this radical form of belief from atheism. Atheists, on the whole, find no use for the traditions and practices of religion. For many, if not most in the Network, religious faith is, at the very least, a valuable resource and inspiration for living, even if its institutions and practices are in need of radical reform. "Non-realist" was important to those who wanted to set their approach to faith in the context of a broader cultural and philosophical shift.

The atheist and the realist would agree in seeing at the heart of their disagreement about faith the question of God's existence. The non-realist's strategy is to undermine this very question and thereby challenge the believer and non-believer to come to a common understanding. To undermine the atheist and realist's question, the non-realist draws attention to the human creativity not only at the heart of religious faith but at the heart of all human knowledge and understanding, even at the heart of our knowledge and understanding of our very selves. We make our world through the language that we cannot help but use to talk about it. We make ourselves through the stories of our lives. The challenge to the believer and non-believer alike is to recognise that if everything – our knowledge, our truth, our faith and our selves – springs from human communities, then our truth and our knowledge are related to the goals of those communities and the quality of relationships within them.

The ambitions of the non-realist strategy are revolutionary. Such a strategy offers the hope of bringing about the coalition between believers and non-believers that Hans Küng argues is necessary for the creation of a world ethic. "Without religious peace", he writes, "there is no world peace." Faith seen as a human creation offers common ground for believer and non-believer alike. Seeing God as rising from the heart of human community offers the hope of undermining the inequalities upon which present reality and human relationships are built. Stripping away all traces of supernaturalism places the responsibility for justice and the relief of suffering firmly in our hands.

All these themes have been explored in an outpouring of writing by Don Cupitt in some sixteen books published since *The Sea of Faith* in 1984. These have culminated in a trilogy of *Religion in Everyday Speech* books. They open up the possibility of a further important and cultural hope for Sea of Faith religion.

In the mid-1980s, according to the *General Household Survey*, 5 per cent of the UK population attended the theatre, opera or ballet while 98 per cent were watching television on average for over 25 hours a week. Two per cent of all young people were attending the theatre and 40 per cent of 16–24 year olds were going to the cinema at least every three months. Commenting on these statistics at the beginning of the 1990s, Paul Willis wrote:

The institutions and practices, genres and terms of high art are currently categories of exclusion more than inclusion. They have no real connection with most young people or their lives … (Willis 1990:1)

These figures remain largely unchanged at the end of the twentieth century. The institutions of religious faith would appear to have more in common with those of high art than those of popular culture. They too could be said to have little connection with most young people or their lives. But while the cultural statistics remain broadly unchanged, the 1980s and 1990s have also seen continued and rapid globalisation of transnational industry, the worldwide web and digital communications. If the class divisions of "high brow" and "low brow" have given way to "high art" and the "popular", a consumerist "mass culture" now penetrates deep into the heart of cultural identities of all kinds. A diversity of all forms of life now jostle together bringing both extraordinary vitality and deep insecurity.

Where once religion, a word deriving from the Latin "to bind", was that which bound its people together, that role has largely been taken over by culture. The similarities run deep. Habits, customs, language and feelings bind us, in part unconsciously, to our ways of life. But while so much of our belief and identity is reflected unconsciously in our behaviour, so too we speak of our culture as the most highly prized creation of our reflection and creativity. Terry Eagleton summarises a form of the "Culture/culture" problem that arises.

> How can culture be at once what we don't need to think about, and the finest fruits of our consciousness? If religion, or high culture, is rooted in culture as a way of life, then it risks being reducible to it, and its transcendent value is accordingly lost. Yet if it does not have such everyday roots, how can it be effective? (Eagleton 2000:115)

T. S. Eliot was quite clear that culture for most people would remain a ritual of unconscious conformism. There could be no question, for him, of any direct offering of the values of the minority to the masses:

> … to make everyone share in the apprehension of the fruits of the more conscious part of the culture is to adulterate and cheapen what you give. (Eliot 1948:106)

This is the kind of elitism that kept the theological reflection of the theological college and university department away from the lay people in the pew. It contrasts sharply with Raymond Williams' vision of a common culture where there is a collaborative making of shared meanings and values, with full participation of all its members and a growing advance in consciousness.

Broadcasting *The Sea of Faith* and publishing *God in Us* challenged an elitist view of faith. Now the challenge runs even deeper. For just as a thriving common culture must have roots in the common soil of the everyday so too must religious faith. Just as full participation in a culture demands a growing advance in consciousness, so too religious faith must become self-aware. This radical demand involves more than a reflection and reinterpretation of the faith. Faith must find its energy in the ordinary, common language, habits and customs of everyday life.

In the foreword of the first of his latest trilogy of Everyday Speech books, Cupitt challenges the sort of elitism portrayed by Eliot:

Ordinary-language, or "democratic" philosophy has often been discussed during the past half-century, but hardly anyone has ventured to practise it. No doubt people have been influenced by the old assumption that without the controlling influence of academic "disciplines" and church authorities, the thought of ordinary people must be disorderly, superstitious and lacking in serious intellectual interest.

This essay aims to overthrow that assumption. I collect, analyse and interpret a substantial body of new idioms that have recently become established in the language, with the aim of demonstrating in them a surprisingly coherent, interesting and up-to-date religious philosophy of life. It turns out that ordinary language is the best radical theologian and significantly sharper than the professionals. Furthermore, establishment in the common language is the most important and powerful kind of establishment there is. (Cupitt 1999)

Cupitt is surprised by what he discovers. Recent changes in the use and meaning of the word "life" amount to a major religious event. Here is a faith that embraces new incarnations in the everyday world of ordinary life and offers the hope of finally collapsing the distinction between the sacred and the secular, the earthly and the heavenly, the human and the divine.

PROLOGUE

Don Cupitt

When I was a young National Service officer in the army in the mid-1950s, I had the chance to observe the regular officers in the mess. They fell into two classes. The commanding officer, the adjutant, and two or three ambitious junior officers were true believers, permanently full of boyish enthusiasm for leading men and getting on with the job, whatever it was. The rest were a mixed bunch of captains and "flapper majors" – men who had reached their career limit. They were good-humoured and did an adequate job, but they were a little ironical. They were not one hundred per cent committed, and it was somehow obvious.

I preferred the company of the flapper majors (an odd expression that sticks in the memory) because they were much more interesting to talk to. It struck me that every profession was like this, and that I myself could never really be happy as one of the True Believers. I would have to be someone like a writer or an artist, who follows a solitary path. And so it turned out, for when in the early 1970s I was offered my own chances of high office, first in the church, and then later in the academy, I turned them down with only the briefest hesitation – and within a year or two had burnt my boats by publishing ideas that put me permanently out of the running anyway.

All of which goes to show that in the end I brought my troubles upon myself, and cannot complain about the way things have turned out. I always knew that at the end of my life I would not be content to look back and say: "I was a loyal servant of the System, and the System duly honoured me for it." I would only be happy if I could feel that I had come out and said in full whatever I had it in me to say. In personal ethics, expressive freedom is the first value of all. Our first task is to become ourselves, and we do it by expressing ourselves.

This explains my cautious reaction in 1986 or so, when I was first approached by the founding group about what was to become Sea of Faith. I did not want us in any way to repeat the old relationship of shepherd and sheep, guru and disciples, leader and followers. Under today's conditions, neither party gains from such a relationship. I'd be the loser if I were to get caught up in a "political" situation that constrained me always to say not what *I* needed to say, but what the troops needed to hear. I remembered Nietzsche's Zarathustra, looking over his shoulder and saying to his would-be followers: "Don't follow me: follow yourselves!" In those late-80s days the leading London art colleges were fizzing with the burst of talent and new ideas that was to give rise to Young British Art, and I was already saying that the church of the future would need to be less like a well-disciplined army, and more like an art college. Old-style church Christianity, with its standardised and legally binding forms of belief, worship and practice, nowadays *diminishes* people. What we will need in the future are religious forms that make people *bigger,* not smaller – which means that we need to create the first really free religious society; a society that doesn't inhibit its own members, but actively encourages each member to find and to develop his or her own voice.

The most encouraging thing about Sea of Faith so far is the extent to which it has already begun to fulfil these hopes. We are perhaps not as numerous as we hoped to be by this stage, we are perhaps a bit elderly, and we are too easily marginalised by those who see us as a threat. But the excellent essays collected in this book – about half by members, and half by fellow-travellers and sympathetic outsiders – show clearly that the "idea" of Sea of Faith is catching on and is beginning to mean something to people. Sea of Faith already has its own new sort of identity and sense of belonging.

The shift we have made is a very big one. Amongst the Western half of humankind, monotheistic religion and political monarchy have long combined to persuade us that the strongest society is a society whose members are united by their common state of unconditional subjection to One Absolute Lord. To this day many people expect the best religion to be the most uncompromisingly authoritarian, and demand that the Ark of Salvation be run as the very tightest of tight ships. And despite all the ideas about human freedom, liberal democracy and human rights that have developed since the Enlightenment, authoritarianism is still felt by many people to be perfectly natural in the spheres of morality and religion. An objective authority and objective reality are felt to be needed in order to tame wild and disorderly human nature.

Nevertheless, that whole mentality is coming to an end today, and a vivid indicator of the change is a line from Nietzsche, written as early as the 1880s: "All of us are no longer material for a society." What he means is this: it's too late for socialism and it's too late to ask normal people for unconditional commitment to any one society or religion or philosophy of life, because we now know too much. We are all of us a bit ironical, like the flapper majors, because we cannot help being aware of other political systems, other world-views, other beliefs – and also, of historical change. Modern human beings cannot commit themselves unconditionally and for life to just one framework of beliefs and values and one social role, because we know too well how much things change during a single lifetime and how much we will want to change with them. We are all a bit plural and a bit free-flowing nowadays – and *that's* why we need a new kind of religious society that allows people the freedom to change and develop. The old kind of society, highly aware of the violence and unruliness of human beings, set out to hold them within a very strict disciplinary framework: the more rigid the framework, the stronger the society seemed to be. Typically, you took life vows and you stayed in one place for life. But the strength of the newer kind of society will consist in its very loose-knit and elastic character: it will allow people all the room they need for self-expression and for growth. People will be held together, not by their being in a common state of subjection to power, but by their respect for each other's spiritual freedom.

I still believe that Sea of Faith at its best offers a first draft of the church of the future – the first truly liberating church. Alternatively, we may see the change we are making as a move away from the old disciplinary and dualistic church-Christianity towards the more relaxed kingdom-religion of the future.

This kingdom-religion will be undogmatic, and I have space here to make only one point about it, by following up the theme of Patti Whaley's essay on "Religion and Human Rights". In the Western tradition that went back through the Enlightenment to Aquinas, human rights were commonly spoken of as if they were natural facts created by God. Philosophers took a realist view of rights as things "out there", and even solemnly argued about their "existence". But in recent years people who have studied the history of (for example) workers' rights, or women's rights, have come to take an historical view of human rights. Each of my rights is a socially-agreed and entrenched limit upon the power of some other person or group to muck me about. Each right is a human creation: the precious legacy to us of those forebears of ours who first battled for it and eventually managed to get it recognised and built into socially-authoritative laws and customs.

This newer, historical view of human rights is of course non-realistic. Rights don't exist "out there". Rights are just conventional. Brave pioneering human beings saw the need for them, formulated them, and battled to get them publicly acknowledged. And along these lines we may gradually come to see our whole moral tradition as a slowly accumulating human creation.

But that doesn't mean that it's any less important to us! It is surely obvious that one can *both* hold the correct, non-realistic view of what a human right is – namely, an historically-established human convention – *and* also maintain that human rights matter very much indeed to us. And the same applies to religious beliefs and ideas. In the church the popular view is that non-realism about God is the same thing as "atheism", which is exactly like saying that unless you think that human rights are metaphysical facts you must reject them altogether and be as wicked a person as the late Pol Pot. But that is a mistaken view. What the non-realist is saying is simply that we should give up the idea that in our morality and our religion we are describing and holding on to bodies of timeless metaphysical facts. Instead, we should see both our moral tradition and our religious tradition as historically evolving human creations. Since World War Two we have done rather well in developing and adding to our *moral* tradition, but our religious traditions lag horribly far behind, held up by various realistic illusions. Sea of Faith shows how religion might begin to grow again – and so help us to grow, too. I still think that it's the best prospect available, and am grateful for the witness of this book's contributors to it.

GOD AND THE FUTURE

Karen Armstrong

The Sea of Faith Network was founded to meet the growing conviction that the God of Western classical theism is dead and can no longer give men and women the sense of transcendence and ecstasy they seek and need. In 1882 Friedrich Nietzsche had imagined a madman running into the marketplace looking frantically for God. When the amused bystanders asked where he thought God had gone – had he taken a vacation, perhaps, or emigrated? – the madman glowered at them. "Where has God gone?" he demanded. "We have killed him, you and I. We are his murderers!" As a result, humanity had lost its basic orientation. "Do we not stray," the madman asked in despair, "as though through an infinite nothingness?"

In one sense, the twentieth century has proved Nietzsche wrong. Since the 1970s, religion has once again become a factor in public life in a way that would once have seemed inconceivable. The Iranian revolution was succeeded by an eruption of Islamic revivalism in the Middle East; at about the same time, the Moral Majority tried to bring God back into public life in the United States, while ultra-Orthodox Jews and radical religious Zionists have done the same in Israel. Now no government can safely ignore religion. The assassinations of Anwar Sadat in Egypt and Yitzak Rabin in Israel are sober reminders of the lethal dangers of some forms of modern faith. But it is also true that fundamentalism has endorsed Nietzsche's prophecy: it can be seen as a desperate attempt to resuscitate God. Fundamentalists certainly believe that modern society has tried to kill God. Every single radical religious movement that I have studied has been inspired by a profound fear of annihilation. Rightly or wrongly, fundamentalists in all three of the Abrahamic faiths are convinced that the secularist establishment wants to wipe them out; and they have decided to fight back.

But in Europe we have little fundamentalism, properly so called. In London, churches are being converted into restaurants, art galleries, theatres and restaurants. Only 6 per cent of the population of Britain attend a religious service regularly, and to profess an allegiance to any faith is becoming increasingly eccentric. Yet I think it would be a mistake to assume that there is no interest in spirituality or no hunger for the sacred. People may reject traditional ideas about God but the quest to find some ultimate meaning and value in life continues. Religion is natural to human beings. It has not been imposed upon us by authoritarian priests and kings; it is something that we have always done. We are creatures that constantly seek ecstasy, a word whose original meaning was "to go beyond the self". It is one of the peculiarities of the human mind that it has experiences and conceives ideas that transcend it. In an ecstatic experience, we feel most fully alive, lifted momentarily beyond ourselves and touched profoundly within. We feel in contact with the deeper currents of existence. Religion has been one of the chief outlets of transcendence, but there are others, and when people no longer find ecstasy in a synagogue, church or mosque, they seek it in art, music, sex or drugs.

We need this ecstasy because we are beings who fall very easily into despair. We are the only animals that have to live with the knowledge of our mortality, and we find this vision of extinction hard to bear. Religion has always been one of the ways whereby men and women have come to terms with the baffling and tragic world in which they find themselves. As soon as we became recognisably human, we created religions at the same time – and for many of the same reasons as we created works of art. Our art and religious symbols encouraged us to look beneath the surface of existence and to encounter a dimension that went beyond our normal experience. Both helped people to see the world anew, to hold themselves in an attitude of wonder and to cultivate the conviction that against all the dispiriting evidence to the contrary, life had some ultimate meaning and value. Religion does not merely mean the acceptance of certain dogmas, nor does it require adherence to a supernatural order. Buddhism, for example, does not accept the notion of the supernatural and can be called a religion without "God". Religion and faith consist rather in the struggle for a meaning that will prevent us from falling into the crippling despondency to which humanity is prone.

We are meaning-seeking creatures and need to engage in an effort to find some shape and pattern in our otherwise amorphous existence. But the great traditions have always insisted that the ultimate pattern must always transcend human categories that elude our human comprehension. Our paradigms can only point to a dimension that exists ineffably and incomprehensibly beyond them. Indeed, an essential part of our human experience of life has been the apprehension of "something" that transcends it. We seek out experiences of this kind. But the forms and symbols of religion must change. Our sense of life's meaning can only be satisfied in ways that speak to our particular situation. Each generation has had to wrest its own interpretation or revelation from the past and force it to address a modernity that its original proponents could not have imagined. But our own modernity is different from any other and will therefore require even more radical reinterpretation of tradition. In the West we have evolved a society that depends not on an agrarian surplus (as did all pre-modern civilisations) but on technology. We have developed a scientific outlook that demands a certain dissociation of sensibility, a highly literal reading of texts, and a specialisation and compartmentalisation of experience. Our secularism, the attempt to separate religion from politics and to confine it to its own distinct and privatised sphere, is an unprecedented experiment. In these radically altered circumstances, it is no wonder that the old religious symbols of our ancestors no longer work for us. Our religious experience has changed. We read our scriptures in a wholly different way from our pre-modern ancestors, and have evolved different criteria of truth.

One of the problems is that in the Western world we have fallen into the habit of imagining that our notion of God is an objective, demonstrable fact – similar to the phenomena we investigate in our laboratories. Formed in a scientific world, we interpret our scriptures literally, in a way that would have seemed strange to the most eminent of our Jewish, Christian and Muslim forebears. The familiarity with scripture, which some more conventional Christians evince, and the ease with which they quote texts at one another, would have been impossible before the invention of printing enabled everybody to own his own Bible, or before the widespread literacy which is unique to our modernity enabled her to read it. There is also a common conviction that "God" must be a reality whose existence can be proved, even though the traditions all insist that the Sacred is ineffable and indescribable. It cannot be confined within any doctrinal system, however august. To explain or to rationalise our experience of the divine will kill it, just as heavy-handed literary criticism can destroy the grace of a poem.

When we speak about God, Brahman or Nibbana, all the traditions assert, we are at the end of what thoughts and words can do. But the traditions are also clear that while "God" cannot be reached by the logic of rational thought, the sense of the Sacred has to be cultivated, in rather the same way as we cultivate an aesthetic sensibility. God is not a reality that we can experience as simply as we see a book or hear a motorcar. We have to learn to look beneath the surface of the mundane to glimpse this dimension, to see through the unpromising outward shell to its sacred core. This requires practice. If somebody who had never seen a single piece of Western art wandered into an art gallery in London or New York, he would be unlikely to be moved by the paintings of

Cézanne or Picasso. It is difficult to listen to the music of another culture, because we have different expectations of melody and harmony. But even though we know that we have to work at aesthetics, learning to educate our eyes and ears, we do not always appreciate that a sense of the divine also takes time and hard work, requiring the same stringency and dedication as a gift for mathematics or playing the piano.

It is no good expecting to "see" this sacred dimension of existence with normal mundane consciousness. The churches do people a disservice when they speak as though God were an obvious fact of life. Theology should not be a simple statement of fact; it should move us in the same way as a great poem; our liturgy should yield a sense of transcendence in the same way as good theatre. These aesthetic forms, if handled with creativity, ingenuity, discipline and skill can move, exalt, inspire and help people to look through the confusions of daily life and have intimations of sacredness. But all too often, theology and liturgy are mechanical, boring and as ineffective as bad art.

But above all, the traditions insist, it is essential that we abandon egotism and selfishness if we wish to have an experience of the divine. We are most fully ourselves when we give ourselves away. It is ego that diminishes us, limits our vision and has been found to be incompatible with the Sacred. But it is very hard to rid ourselves of selfishness. Much of what passes for religion is in fact an endorsement of the egotism we are supposed to transcend in the ecstasy of faith. People want their prayers answered; they want to "get to heaven". We feel good about being "right", and our religion can make us feel superior to unbelievers. Even members of the Sea of Faith Network can feel that they are more advanced than traditional believers. When we are working hard to get rid of the ego, we can fall into a form of narcissism. Egotism is so pervasive that it is hard to lay it aside. But, the religions insist in different ways, until we do so we will not glimpse the divine, but only a reflection of ourselves. The grain of wheat has to fall into the ground and die if it is to bear fruit (John 12:24). The word *Islam* means surrender. One of the first things that the Prophet Muhammad made his converts do was to prostrate themselves several times a day in prayer. This was difficult for the Bedouin, who were averse to kingship and found it appalling to grovel on the ground like slaves, but the physical abasement taught them at a level deeper than the cerebral to abandon the limitations of the posturing ego, which is so protective of our pride, interests, identity, survival and status. The struggle for survival in a flawed and cruel world means that egotism often seems endemic to the human condition. The religions at their best offered a new way of being human. It was, they taught, selflessness and self-abandonment that enabled us to live in what Buddhists called Nibbana and what monotheists called the Presence of God. But because ego is not vanquished in a day, "God" remains elusive.

Like many members of the Sea of Faith Network, I am not dismayed by the widespread atheism of our time. After the genocidal catastrophes we witnessed during the twentieth century, many of the old ideas about God have come to seem facile and incoherent. Atheism can represent a rejection of inadequate notions of the divine and a refusal to find a facile solution to the difficulty and darkness that falls upon the human spirit when contemplating Auschwitz, Hiroshima, Bosnia and Rwanda. Historically, the word "atheism" was used to describe the rejection of a particular conception of the divine, not to denote a blanket rejection of the Sacred *in toto*. The word "atheism" has also been used during periods of transition, when people were making a new leap forward in religious understanding. Thus at an early stage of their history, Jews, Christians and Muslims were all called "atheists" by their pagan contemporaries, not because they did not believe in God, but because their conception of the divine was so radically different from current notions as to seem blasphemous. Monotheists have always been concerned with idolatry, the worship of human images of the divine. This can apply just as easily to a theology as to an effigy of a false deity. It may be that the atheism we see will also herald the advent of a new form of religious understanding. In a restaurant, when we have eaten a strong-tasting first course, we are sometimes given a sorbet to cleanse our palates so that we can appreciate what follows. Many people today may feel the need to rinse their minds of inadequate, lazy or outmoded theology and wait for a while in what the mystics used to call the Cloud of Unknowing or the Dark Night of the Soul. The Greek Orthodox theologians (in Gregory of Nyssa's *Life of Moses* and Denys the Areopagite's *Mystical Theology)* used to quote the story of Moses going up the mountain to meet God; the summit was enveloped in cloud; he could see nothing but he was in the place where God was. If we think, as I believe we should, of theology as poetry, an exercise of the creative imagination, we can learn from the experience of John Keats, who spoke of the state of "negative capability" which was, he said, necessary for the creation of the best poetry, "when a man is capable of being in uncertainties, mysteries, doubts, without any irritable reaching after fact and reason" (letter to George and Thomas Keats, December 21, 1817). Modern theologians could emulate Keats's ability to wait, glimpsing "only particles of light in the midst of a great darkness – without knowing the bearing of any one assertion of any one opinion" (letter to George and Georgiana Keats, March 19, 1819).

But is there anything we can do while we are waiting in this darkness – an attitude that is hard for modern people who are used to the instant communication of the e-mail. I believe that there is. All the great world faiths insist that the crucial test of any theology or spiritual practice is that it results in practical compassion. If your vision of God makes you kind, patient and selfless, it is good theology. If it makes you bigoted, self-righteous, contemptuous of other people's faith or dismissive of others, it is bad theology. But I have come to believe that compassion is more than a test of faith. It is itself creative of a sense of God. The Buddha used to urge monks and lay people to sit quietly, radiating thoughts of compassion, benevolence and sympathy to all four corners of the world, not excluding a single creature from this radius of love (Anguttara Nikaya 3:65). Thus they would know *ceto-vimutti* (release of the mind), a phrase that in the Buddhist scriptures is an equivalent for the attainment of the supreme enlightenment and Nibbana. Why? Because a habit of universal compassion breaks down the carapace of egotism that holds us back from our best selves and the experience of the Sacred. It dethrones the self and puts others in the centre of our lives, giving us an ecstasy that transcends the limitations of our ordinary existence, liberates us from personal likes and dislikes, does not permit us the selfishness of antipathy, and prevents us from seeing others from a viewpoint of self-interest. This will introduce us to the infinity of Nibbana, or to what, perhaps, monotheists used to call the Divine Presence. As an early Buddhist hymn puts it: "May our loving thoughts fill the whole world, above, below, across, without limit; a boundless goodwill towards the whole world, unrestricted, free of hatred and enmity" (Sutta Nipata, 118).

A key text is the Golden Rule of Rabbi Hillel, an older contemporary of Jesus, who summed up the entire teaching of Judaism in the maxim: "Do not do unto others as you would not have done unto you. That is the Torah. The rest is commentary. Go and learn it" (Shabbat, 31A). It is an extraordinary summary of Judaism: there is no mention of God. But I believe that God is at the heart of the Golden Rule, which Jesus also taught in another form (Matthew 7:12). If every time we are about to say something unpleasant about a colleague, a rival institution, a religion, or another race, and ask ourselves how we should like such a thing said about ourselves, and then refrain from the remark, we would for that moment have transcended egotism. Living in such a way on a daily, hourly basis, we should achieve that constant ecstasy that does not consist of exotic states of consciousness but which brings us into the ambit of sacredness.

This is an insight found in one of the earliest passages of the Bible. Jews, Christians and Muslims all revere Abraham as the father of faith, but from the Biblical account it is hard to discover what Abraham actually believed. He seems to have little of the certainty that we associate with faith today. He is constantly in the dark, asking God questions to which no satisfactory answers are forthcoming. But he did have one fulfilling religious experience (Genesis 18). Sitting outside his tent at Mamre in the hottest part of the day, he saw three strangers on the horizon. Strangers in the ancient Middle East, as in our own society, were potentially dangerous. Very few of us would bring three total strangers off the street and into our own home. But that is what Abraham did. He brought them into his encampment, prepared an elaborate meal, and gave to these three strangers all the comfort he could to refresh them on their journey. And in the course of the ensuing conversation, it transpires that one of these strangers is Abraham's God. The act of practical compassion led to a divine encounter. It is of the utmost importance that the recipients of Abraham's kind act were strangers. In Hebrew the word for "holy" is *qaddosh* (separate, other). The shock of strangeness, the baffling otherness of somebody who does not belong to our ethnic or ideological group can give us intimations of the Otherness or Holiness that we call "God".

Today we often assume that we must first work out our metaphysical beliefs and convince ourselves about "God" before we begin to live in a religious way. This is a good scientific and modern principle: first you establish a principle and only then can you apply it. But in fact the religious traditions work the other way around. First we live compassionately and only then will we glimpse the Sacredness that gives meaning to our lives. While we puzzle about the existence or non-existence of God or the reality or non-realism of the divine, we could do well to practise the compassion taught by all the major traditions, while waiting in the Cloud of Unknowing. We could also bear in mind the poem of William Blake called "The Divine Image":

> *To Mercy, Pity, Peace and Love*
> *All pray in their distress;*
> *And to these virtues of delight*
> *Return their thankfulness.*

For Mercy, Pity, Peace and Love
Is God our father dear,
And Mercy, Pity, Peace and Love
Is Man, his child and care.

For Mercy has a human heart,
Pity a human face,
And Love, the human form divine,
And Peace, the human dress.

Then every man, of every clime,
That prays in his distress,
Prays to the human form divine,
Love, Mercy, Pity, Peace.

And all must love the human form,
In heathen Turk or Jew;
Where Mercy, Love and Pity dwell
There God is dwelling too.

THE JEWISH ISLAND OF DISBELIEF

Dan Cohn-Sherbok

It might come as a surprise for members of the Sea of Faith to learn that in the American Jewish community there currently exist two important movements that reject the belief in a supernatural deity. Despite their radicalism, both Reconstructionist Judaism and Humanistic Judaism are widely perceived as acceptable interpretations of the tradition. Their founders, Mordecai Kaplan and Sherwin Wine, are widely known and their views are not generally condemned as heretical. There is no attempt on the part of the Jewish establishment – embracing both Orthodox Judaism and the non-Orthodox branches of the faith – to stigmatise those who belong to these movements.

Reconstructionist Judaism

Unlike Reform and Conservative Judaism, Reconstructionist Judaism developed out of the thinking of an individual scholar. Born in Lithuania in 1881, Mordecai Kaplan had a traditional Jewish education in Vilna and came to New York City in 1889. After graduating from the City College of New York and the Jewish theological Seminary, he became an associate minister at New York's Orthodox Kehilath Jeshurun. Although officially Orthodox, Kaplan increasingly became disenchanted with traditional Jewish doctrine. In 1910 he became Professor of Homiletics at the Seminary, where he taught philosophy of religion.

According to some scholars, Reconstructionism began as a movement in 1922 when Kaplan initiated a policy of reconstructing Judaism to meet the demands of modern life; others trace its origin to the publication of *Judaism as a Civilization* in 1934. Kaplan himself contended that the movement emerged in 1935 when, as a result of publishing *Judaism as a Civilization*, he and others launched the Reconstructionist magazine. In any event, his book provided the foundation for Reconstructionist ideology.

According to Kaplan, God is not a supernatural being but the power that makes for salvation. "God", he wrote, "is the sum of all the animating, organising forces and relationships which are forever making a cosmos out of chaos". (Kaplan 1970:76) In his view, the idea of God must be understood fundamentally in terms of its effect:

> We learn more about God when we say that love is divine than when we say God is love. A veritable transformation takes place ... Divinity

becomes relevant to authentic experience and therefore takes on a definiteness that is accompanied by an awareness of authenticity. (*Ibid.*:73)

For Kaplan, God is a "trans-natural", "super-factual" and "super-experiential" transcendence, which does not infringe on the law of nature. Such a notion is far removed from the biblical and rabbinic concept of God as the creator and sustainer of the universe who chose the Jewish people and guides humanity to its final destiny.

Turning to the doctrine of revelation, Reconstructionism differs markedly from Orthodoxy. In accordance with the findings of modern biblical scholars who view the Torah as composite, Kaplan stressed that the Bible was not a record of God's dealing with his chosen people; rather it reflected the Jewish search for God. Reconstructionists thus do not regard Jewish law as holy and unchanging. In place of traditional language, Reconstructionists utilise the terms "folkways" and "customs" to designate traditional observances, expressions that reflect the fact that throughout history all peoples have created their sacred events, holy days, and religious objects.

In Kaplan's view, folkways and customs help to sustain the Jewish nation and enrich the spiritual life of Jewry. Yet Kaplan argued that such observances should be accepted voluntarily. There is no role for coercive authority. In this regard, Kaplan endorsed the concept of democratic decision-making in determining which laws are relevant for the community. Further, Kaplan stressed the importance of formulating new customs to take the place of those that had ceased to give meaning to contemporary Jewish life.

Many of the ideas found in *Judaism as a Civilization* were reflected in the religious literature that appeared during this period. The New Haggadah, for example, subordinated the miracles and plagues of the traditional Passover Haggadah to the account of Israel's redemption from Egypt and its significance for both contemporary Judaism and humanity. Similarly, the Sabbath Prayer Book eliminated anachronistic and religiously offensive prayers and all references to the revelation of the Torah on Mount Sinai, the chosenness of Israel, and the doctrine of a personal Messiah.

By the end of the 1960s Reconstructionist Judaism had become a denomination – it established a seminary to train Reconstructionist rabbis and instituted a congregational structure. Regarding halakhah (Jewish law), the Reconstructionist Rabbinical Association issued a statement of its 1980 convention that placed authority in the Jewish people (as opposed to the rabbis) and created a process whereby each congregation would be free to evolve its own minhag (customs). Three years later the Association produced guidelines on intermarriage, encouraging rabbis to welcome mixed couples (a Jew and non-Jew), permit them to participate in Jewish synagogue life, and recognise their children as Jewish if raised as Jews. In addition, the Association decreed that rabbis could sanctify intermarriage as long as it was accompanied by a civil, rather than religious ceremony.

Humanistic Judaism

Humanistic Judaism originated in 1965 when the Birmingham Temple in Detroit, Michigan, began to publicise its philosophy of Judaism. In 1966 a special committee for Humanistic Judaism was organised at the Temple to share service and educational material with rabbis and laity throughout the country. The following year a meeting of several leaders of the movement met in Detroit, issuing a statement that affirmed that Judaism should be governed by empirical reason and human needs; in addition, a new magazine, *Humanistic Judaism*, was founded. In 1969 the Society for Humanistic Judaism was founded in Detroit to provide a basis for co-operation among Humanistic Jews.

In 1986 the International Federation of Secular Humanistic Jews issued a proclamation stating its ideology and aims:

> We believe in the value of human reason and in the reality of the world which reason discloses. The natural universe stands on its own, requiring no supernatural intervention. We believe in the value of human existence and in the power of human beings to solve their problems both individually and collectively. Life should be directed to the satisfaction of human needs. Every person is entitled to life, dignity and freedom. We believe in the value of Jewish identity and in the survival of the Jewish people. Jewish history is a human story. (Cohn-Sherbok 1994:139)

In answer to the question "Who is a Jew", the movement declared:

> We [...] believe that the survival of the Jewish people depends on a broad view of Jewish identity. We welcome into the Jewish people all men and women who sincerely desire to share the Jewish experience regardless of their ancestry. We challenge the assumption that the Jews are primarily or exclusively a religious community and that religious convictions or behaviour are essential to full membership in the Jewish people. (*Ibid.*: 139)

According to the major exponent of Humanistic Judaism, Sherwin Wine, the traditional conception of Jewish history is mistaken. In his view, Abraham, Isaac, and Jacob never existed. Further, the Exodus account is a myth:

> There is no historical evidence to substantiate a massive Hebrew departure from the land of the Pharaohs. As far as we can surmise, the Hebrew occupation of the hill country on both sides of the Jordan was continuous. The twelve tribes never left their ancestral land, never endured 400 years of slavery, and never wandered the Sinai desert. (Wine 1985:35–36)

Moreover, Moses was not the leader of the Hebrews, nor did he compose the Torah. In this light, it is an error to regard the biblical account as authoritative; rather it is a human account of the history of the Israelite nation whose purpose is to reinforce the faith of the Jewish nation.

Like Reconstructionist Judaism, Humanistic Judaism denies any form of supernatural belief. Instead, it regards religious belief as fundamentally psychological in origin. According to the *Guide to Humanistic Judaism*:

> The deity is the projection of the first and most intimate human experience, the dependence of the child on the parents. Patriarchy, monarchy, and traditional religion go hand in hand. Just as the family requires a father-leader and the nation requires a father-king, so does the universe require a father-God. (Society for Humanistic Judaism 1993:27)

Despite such common ground, however, Humanistic Judaism distances itself from Reconstructionism in its use of non-theistic language. Reconstructionist congregations continue to use the religious vocabulary of the past despite the changes that have been made to the liturgy. Humanistic Judaism, however, has jettisoned theistic language. The word "God" has been eliminated from worship. Humanistic prayers are thus radically different from those found in the traditional prayer book. A typical example of such liturgical change is found in the Passover Haggadah. In place of thanksgiving for God's deliverance, Humanistic Jews pray:

> Tonight is a night of memories. Many years ago our fathers were slaves in the land of Egypt. [...] Through the agonies of oppression,

they searched their hearts for one thing that would make life bearable. They searched for hope and found it. They dreamed of freedom and believed that one day it would be theirs. Tonight is a night of hope. (Wine 1988:269)

Like Jewish festivals, life-cycle events have also been reinterpreted in humanistic terms. Unlike traditional Judaism, for example, Humanistic Judaism does not promise eternal life. Rather it accepts the finality of death. According to the *Guide to Humanistic Judaism*, a Humanistic philosophy of death:

> recognises that, although death may be painful and tragic for those who survive and may be profoundly regretted, there is nothing in death to fear, any more than one fears sleeping. One may well be afraid of the pain that may precede death, as one may be afraid of, and would try to avoid, pain generally. But, in the absence of consciousness or feelings after death, there is no reason to fear death itself. (*Ibid.*: 1993:17)

Humanistic Judaism thus offers an option for those who wish to identify with the Jewish community despite their rejection of the traditional understanding of God's nature and activity. Unlike Reconstructionist Judaism, with its emphasis on the observances of the past, Humanistic Judaism fosters a new approach. The Jewish heritage is relevant only in so far as it advances Humanistic ideals. In addition, traditional definitions and principles are set aside in the quest to create a Judaism consonant with a scientific and pluralistic age. Secular in orientation, Humanistic Jews seek to create a world in which the Jewish people are dedicated to the betterment of all humankind.

The Sea of Faith and non-supernatural Judaism

As we have seen, both Reconstructionist and Humanistic Judaism constitute radical departures from the tradition. Their rejection of the fundamental theological presuppositions of the Jewish faith parallels the challenge posed by the Sea of Faith to traditional Christian belief. All three movements endorse a non-supernatural interpretation of religion, emphasising the importance of rational thought. From the Jewish side, Mordecai Kaplan and Sherwin Wine are rabbis and philosophers of religion; similarly Don Cupitt is a priest and philosopher. All three figures are charismatic leaders with a following of devoted disciples.

Yet, there are important differences between these Jewish movements and the Sea of Faith Network. Unlike the Sea of Faith, which is a small society with relatively few members, Reconstructionist Judaism is one of the major branches of Judaism in the United States. The movement has established its own rabbinical college in Philadelphia, and has ordained over 100 men and women for the rabbinate. These graduates serve as rabbis and educators in Reconstructionist congregations throughout the United States.

In the 1950s the Reconstructionist Rabbinic Fellowship consisted of about a hundred Conservative and Reform rabbis sympathetic to the philosophy of Reconstructionism; its aims were to encourage creative synagogue worship and education as well as the establishment of local and national organic communities. With the founding of the Reconstructionist Rabbinical College, an association of Reconstructionist rabbinical alumni was established, and in 1975 its first conference was held. Six years later it began to publish its own journal. In the sphere of liturgy, the Reconstructionist movement has actively encouraged the creation of a wide range of liturgical material. While retaining much of the traditional liturgy, this material altered various aspects of the liturgy in accord with Reconstructionist ideology.

Although Humanistic Judaism is much smaller than Reconstructionism, it is an international organisation with branches throughout the Jewish world. The National Federation currently comprises nine national organisations in the United States, Canada, Britain, France, Belgium, Israel, Australia, Argentina and Uruguay.

In recent years, the movement has founded a Humanistic rabbinical programme, and in 1999 the first rabbi was ordained. In the area of liturgy, Humanistic Judaism has produced a variety of liturgical material reflecting the ideology of the movement. Unlike Reconstructionist Judaism, Humanistic prayer books eliminate any reference to God and emphasise the importance of humanistic values. Thus the Sabbath is viewed as a day of peace, restoration and study. Above all it is a time to affirm and celebrate Jewish identity. Like the adherents of the other branches of contemporary Judaism, Humanistic Jews also view the New Year as spiritually significant. Humanistic Judaism, however, focuses on the role of self-evaluation rather than divine judgment. The three Pilgrim Festivals – Passover, Sukkot and Shavuot – also have important significance for Humanistic Jews. Passover, for example, teaches the valuable lesson of liberation; it extols the quest for freedom in a variety of readings commemorating this pivotal event in the history of the nation.

Despite the objections of traditionalists to these radical interpretations of the tradition, Reconstructionist and Humanistic Judaism have become part of mainstream Judaism. Their rabbis and organisational structures have been absorbed into American Jewish life. The Sea of Faith, on the other hand, is at the margins of Christian community, and it is frequently vilified by the Christian establishment. Some of its members – particularly those ordained to the priesthood or ministry – seek to keep their sympathies secret, fearful of evoking an adverse reaction. Unlike Mordecai Kaplan, who is widely regarded as one of the major Jewish thinkers of the modern age, Don Cupitt is often criticised and frequently misunderstood.

How can one account for these differences? One of the central features of the modern Jewish community is its ethnic, as opposed to religious, character. In the past Judaism was an essentially monolithic tradition based on a universal acceptance of the binding character of the Torah. Living an isolated existence, Jews were loyal to their religious heritage in the face of gentile hostility. Today, however, the Jewish community has fragmented into a variety of religious denominations with conflicting ideologies and lifestyles. In addition, there are currently many Jews – including those in Israel – who are entirely secular in orientation. Hence, religious doctrine has become far less important in the Jewish world than in the Christian community.

It must be remembered, in this connection, that Jewish identity is not based on either belief or practice. According to traditional Judaism, a person is Jewish if he or she has a Jewish mother. It makes no difference if that individual adheres to the central tenets of the Jewish faith, or is religiously observant. In recent years, a number of non-Orthodox movements have expanded this criterion of Jewishness to include patrilineal as well as matrilineal descent. This means that anyone born of either a Jewish mother or father is perceived as Jewish. Thus birth, rather than belief or practice, serves as the determining factor in establishing who is a Jew. While conversion to Judaism is permitted, most Jews are Jewish by virtue of descent.

In this light it is understandable why the Jewish community is generally tolerant of non-theistic modes of Jewish existence. Reconstructionist and Humanistic Jews are not anathematised because of their convictions. What matters far more is their loyalty to the Jewish heritage and their identification with the community. In this respect, Reconstructionist and Humanistic Jews – despite their departures from the tradition – are perceived as supporters of Jewish institutional life. What matters is their concern to ensure that Judaism in some form continues to animate Jewish life in a changing world.

The Sea of Faith, on the other hand, is widely perceived by the Christian community as a threat to the faith. Unlike Judaism, Christianity is based on religious conviction rather than maternal or paternal descent. For the vast majority of Christians, it simply makes no sense to identify oneself as a Christian while simultaneously denying the central tenets of the creed. Hence, most traditionalist Christians have no sympathy for a non-realist interpretation of Christianity. The Sea of Faith is therefore frequently branded as an organisation of "Godless vicars" or "atheist priests".

In defence, the Sea of Faith declares that it is simply an informal network of men and women who accept the modern view that all religious traditions are wholly human creations. But rather than placating its detractors, such statements inflame those Christians who insist that the Christian faith is based on an acceptance of such doctrines as the Incarnation and the Trinity. Here there is a crucial parting of the ways between contemporary Judaism and Christianity. In general, Jews are tolerant of non-supernatural forms of Judaism, whereas the Christian community is united in its condemnation of non-realism.

Conclusion

As we have seen, non-theistic interpretations of the Jewish faith have become part of the mainstream of American Jewish life. Arguably this is to be expected, given the murder of six million Jews in the Holocaust. Increasingly Jews have found it difficult to believe in an all-good and omnipotent deity, given God's seeming absence at Auschwitz. If God chose the Jews, loves them, and providentially guides their destiny, why did he allow innocent victims to die in the most tragic fashion at the hands of the Nazis? This searing theological question forms the background to the shift in consciousness that has taken place in the Jewish community. Although many Jews continue to believe in the God of scripture, others find such convictions incomprehensible. As we have noted, Christians will find it much more difficult to take leave of God. Yet the emergence of these two non-supernatural movements within the Jewish community should offer inspiration to members of the Sea of Faith. One looks forward to the day when Don Cupitt, like Mordecai Kaplan and Sherwin Wine, will be regarded as a spiritual pioneer of the modern age.

THE INGENIOUSLY ORDERED UNIVERSE

Paul Davies

Don Cupitt is undoubtedly one of the most exciting theologians of our era. His bold reformulation of theology is a welcome attempt to bring a fresh new perspective to religion and its place in the broader scheme of human intellectual enquiry. In particular, I applaud his attempt to reappraise traditional theological concepts in the light of post-modern thought and our new understanding of the role of language and culture in shaping our world view. Where I must part company with Cupitt, however, is in his denial of "a stable, mind-independent world order out there" (Cupitt, 1997:72). I take issue with this position on both scientific and theological grounds.

I write first and foremost as a scientist. The thesis I wish to defend is that scientific knowledge of the world is in a class apart from other forms of knowledge, and that while Cupitt's deconstructionist arguments have some force when applied to other belief systems (religion, folklore, history, social theory …) they are less convincing when directed at science.

Cupitt is by no means alone in deploying post-modern and deconstructionist critiques to science. It has become fashionable to characterise science as just another culturally-relative set of myths that certain people (scientists) hold about the world, myths that have no greater or lesser claim on our allegiance than alternative belief systems (e.g. magic, shamanism, Aboriginal dreaming). Because science is largely a product of Western European thought, attempts have been made to present it as a culturally-laden, Eurocentric, male-oriented activity, and as such subject to the cultural prejudices and world view of that restricted class. While it is undeniable that the scientific agenda and the professional practices of scientists reflect the cultural baggage of the practitioners, I contend that the actual *fruits* of science should not be viewed in that light.

Science proceeds from three basic assumptions:

1. There exists a real world "out there". That is to say, however much our human psychology and sensory apparatus may distort our view of things, there exists some sort of objective reality called "nature" or "the universe". Our observations of the physical world reflect, albeit imperfectly, a really-existing system.

2. The physical universe is ordered in a rational way.
3. The order in nature is at least in part intelligible to us.

It would not be possible to be a scientist without supposing that there is a really-existing order in nature. If you believed that this order was merely imposed upon nature by human concepts and culture, science would be reduced to a charade. In other words, scientists suppose that we read order out of nature, not into nature. To take a concrete example, I maintain that Newton's inverse square law of gravity describes a real property of nature, e.g. that the gravitational force on a body transported twice as far from the sun is reduced to one quarter. This is not something that humans have imagined or invented; it is simply true. To be sure, it was discovered by a white European male (Isaac Newton) using mathematics originating in Greece, France and England, but it can be tested empirically by anyone, including female persons from non-European cultures. The inverse square law is a *fact*, pure and simple, and independent of the cultural milieu from which it emerged.

Conditions 2 and 3 are in a different category. The universe does not have to be ordered, but if it were not, we should not be here to worry about it. The job of the scientist is to unveil that (really-existing) order in nature, using a mixture of rational reasoning and experimentation. Rationality is important here, for if the universe were absurd or arbitrary, science could make no progress. I shall return to this point later.

There is no *a priori* reason why human beings should be able to do science. It is easy to imagine a universe that is ordered, but in a way that is either too subtle or too complicated for human beings to grasp. The fact that we can come to understand the physical universe through science to such an amazing degree is one of the great outstanding mysteries of metaphysics, and one that some commentators at least have interpreted as evidence for something like design or purpose in nature. Thus point 3, the intelligibility of the world, is in no way logically necessary for the existence of a rational world containing observers. It is, however, necessary if such a world is to contain scientists, for it would be pointless to embark on the path of science without some assurance that one will thereby be able to comprehend (in part) the processes of nature under investigation. Thus, though scientists have no need of God to explain the actual operation of the universe, science itself is not without an element of faith, because to be a scientist you have to believe that nature is ordered in a rational and intelligible manner. Most scientists take the rational intelligibility of the universe for granted, but it actually reflects a distinctively monotheistic world view.

The most important reason that we should take science seriously as a special path to truth is that it works, and works spectacularly well, in a thousand ways. A good example is provided by the subject of light, and its relationship to electricity and magnetism. Human beings have been aware of light, and of electricity at least, since the beginning. What has emerged only in the last 150 years, however, through the efforts of scientists, is that these phenomena are linked. Specifically, light is an electromagnetic wave. Historically, this discovery came about in stages. First, the work of Faraday, Oersted and others established a connection between electricity and magnetism. The connection could be expressed quite precisely as a system of equations. Then in the 1850s James Clerk Maxwell combined the several equations describing the behaviour of electricity, magnetism and their interrelation, and spotted an ugly mathematical inconsistency. He added an extra term to the equations, without any direct experimental evidence for it at the time, and immediately everything fell into place. As a result, Maxwell was able to solve the system of equations, and discover that some solutions corresponded to electromagnetic waves travelling through empty space at a speed that turned out to be identical to that of light. Subsequent experiments confirmed the correctness of his "fudge factor" – the additional mathematical term – plus the fact that light is indeed an electromagnetic wave.

I think it is fair to say that without the thing we call science, human beings would never have discovered this connection between light and electricity, even though both phenomena are very familiar. The power of science is that it can establish links between disparate physical phenomena, and thus provide a deeper understanding of the workings of nature. No other system of thought could achieve this. No amount of magic, ancient folklore, meditation or mystical revelation could arrive at the result Maxwell did. Science tells us things about the world that no other system of thought can even approach. And what it tells us leads to the discovery of things that nobody otherwise knew existed. In the case in hand, the theory went on to predict radio waves, the existence of which had never been suspected before (you can't see or hear them, they pass straight through you without noticeable effect). Similar examples are legion – antimatter, neutrinos, black holes – all these things have been sought and found because scientific theory predicted their existence, which otherwise would have forever gone unsuspected.

It may help to consider a contemporary example. Ultimately the goal of science is to uncover the hidden workings of nature and to make manifest the principles on which the natural order runs. Physics is the archetypal science in this respect, and its language is that of mathematics.

Physicists are not satisfied with a merely descriptive account of natural phenomena. To claim that a theory of such-and-such exists is to display a set of mathematical equations that correctly predicts all aspects of that phenomenon. The foregoing example of Maxwell's equations is a good illustration. Over three centuries of scientific endeavour, the system of equations in mathematical physics has been refined and elaborated. Progress has come from the discovery that the mathematics of nature's disparate phenomena are intertwined; as we have seen, the equations describing electricity and magnetism are connected. In recent decades, further connections have been discovered (e.g. the link between energy and mass encapsulated in Einstein's famous equation $E = mc^2$). Many physicists are currently speculating about a so-called Theory of Everything – a set of equations that would embody all physical phenomena in a single, hopefully simple and elegant, scheme. The idea is that one underlying mathematical structure explains all of nature, so that the different forces of nature, for example, would turn out to be merely different manifestations of a single underlying superforce. (Physicists recognise four fundamental forces: electromagnetism, gravitation and two nuclear forces called weak and strong.) Although it is too soon to know whether this dream of a final unified theory is at hand, superstring theory, and its elaboration called M theory, looks promising.

Along the way to this goal of a final theory, we have a good interim theory that unifies electromagnetism with the weak nuclear force. It involves a key mathematical feature describing a way in which the property of mass might be bestowed upon the participating particles. The relevant mechanism requires the existence of a new subatomic particle with unusual properties, known as the Higgs boson after its proposer, Peter Higgs. Higgs suggested in the 1960s that this particle might be responsible for creating mass. Searches for the Higgs boson have so far failed to discover any such particle. However, physicists believe that this is because it is created only under conditions of very high energy, and that no particle accelerator yet has the punch to make one. My point is this. Does the Higgs boson really exist? If nature is indeed rational and mathematical, and if the semi-unified theory is on the right track, then it ought to be possible to create a Higgs boson in a sufficiently powerful accelerator machine. Such a machine is being built at the CERN particle physics laboratory near Geneva, and in a few years we shall know the answer. If the Higgs boson turns up on cue, then it will provide another dramatic example of the power of science to expose an aspect of reality that would remain forever hidden if human thought had been restricted to non-scientific disciplines.

The Higgs boson is a clear-cut example of the scientist's world view. Either the Higgs boson is real or a figment of physicists' imaginations. It is not some sort of vague, culturally relative concept. A particle is a particle is a particle. If it's there, it will leave a trace in a detector, pure and simple. But we shall have come to know of its existence through the arcane and indirect procedures of science, which recognise that beneath the surface of everyday impressions of the physical universe there is a deep, unifying, mathematical reality. In unveiling that deeper reality, we are in a real sense "glimpsing the mind of God".

In my book *God and the New Physics* I wrote, "science is a surer path to God than religion". At the time I meant these words only semi-seriously; I was trying to be deliberately mischievous. However, given that Cupitt has so successfully deconstructed religion, and argued (convincingly in my opinion) that there is no absolute path from religion to God, then perhaps my words have a greater relevance than I originally intended. In the post-religious world, science is indeed a good place to start in seeking a deeper, meaningful relationship with the universe and its underlying (in my view purposeful) rationality.

Einstein once remarked that the question that most fascinated him was whether God had any choice in the form of his creation. Most scientists agree that the particular law-like order we observe in nature isn't logically necessary. The laws could have been otherwise, or there might have been no laws – or even no universe – at all. The purpose of experimental science is precisely to determine just what the laws are. Judaism, Islam and Christianity are likewise founded on the belief that the universe does not have to be as it is. God was free to order it differently, leave it chaotic, or desist from creating any sort of universe. The observed order is therefore contingent on God.

Science took root in Western Europe under the twin influences of Greek philosophy, with its emphasis on rational reasoning, and the monotheistic religions, which stressed the contingency of nature. The early scientists such as Galileo, Kepler and Newton were deeply religious. They believed that in doing their science they were uncovering God's rational plan for the world. The laws of nature were thoughts in the mind of God, and the mathematical order that those laws express were God's cryptic code. So alongside the scriptures, with their mystical revelations of God, lay "natural theology" – the chance of glimpsing God at work in the order and harmony of the cosmos. Scientists, and physicists especially, still believe that there is a hidden subtext in nature that can be decoded using mathematical procedures and carefully designed experiments.

The obvious question then arises of where the law-like order in nature comes from. Atheists wriggle uncomfortably at this point. Having insisted that everything in the world can be explained rationally in terms of natural laws, when it comes to the origin of the laws themselves a mental back flip is performed: the system of laws must simply be accepted as a brute fact. The laws exist reasonlessly, they say, and at rock bottom the universe is absurd. The glaring contradiction in this argument is that it attempts to ground a logical and rational world in cosmic absurdity.

To escape this trap, some atheists resort to the cosmic selection theory, according to which our universe is merely one among an infinity of different universes. Only in a tiny fraction of these parallel realities will the laws and conditions favour biology and conscious beings. It would then be no surprise that we live in such an ordered universe: we could not survive in most of the others. The trouble with the cosmic selection theory is that it requires an infinity of unseen universes just to explain the one we do see. In this respect it is scarcely an improvement on old-fashioned theism, with its hypothesis of an unseen creator God. Moreover, while the theory may explain why we observe the laws we do, it does not explain why there are universes and laws of some sort in the first place. Perhaps the most telling argument against the many universes theory is that the degree of lawfulness we observe in our universe is far more stringent than is necessary for life. The extraordinary regularities observed in the subatomic realm, for example, have no obvious connection with biology.

However, if the atheist is struggling when it comes to ultimate questions, the theist is no better off. Simply declaring that God made the world and selected a judicious set of laws offers no real explanation at all. It also invites the question of who, or what made God. Unless one can say why God exists, and how God goes about imposing an order on nature, the explanation is vacuous. Since it is a central tenet of Christian theology that God could have made a different universe, the problem of why God made *this* universe is acute. If the choice is arbitrary, we are back with cosmic absurdity. On the other hand, if the choice is determined by God's personal nature, then what decides that nature? Might God have been different too? If God is unique, then God's nature is necessarily as it is, and God's creation is inevitable. But if the universe is inevitable, why do we need God at all?

Clearly both atheistic and theistic arguments collapse in a bewildering tangle of contradictions once we attempt to go beyond the natural world and ask what lies behind physical existence. The problem always occurs when linear reasoning is applied to explanation. Any chain of reasoning has to start somewhere, with certain facts accepted as given, be it God, the universe, the laws of physics, or some logical principle. But for most people the key issue is not which abstract metaphysical argument is the more cogent, but whether the world as revealed by science has a place for meaning and purpose. That is the crux of the matter. Do we live in a universe that came into existence for no reason, and which consists of nothing more than a collection of mindless particles moved by blind and purposeless forces towards a pointless final state? Or is there more to it than that – something deeper, something significant? Is the universe ultimately an absurdity, or is there a solid rational ground to physical existence? In short, is the universe totally meaningless, or is it *about* something?

These are questions that science may not be able to answer, but which it can genuinely illuminate. Take the seemingly arbitrary form of the laws of nature. We can ask whether the observed laws are in any way special or distinctive. The answer is yes. First, the laws of physics marvellously permit the universe to create itself in a big bang, which, in the simplest version of the theory, was the origin of everything – time and space as well as matter and energy. (Augustine was right: the world was made with time, not in time.) This would not be possible with any old laws. The big bang, however, was only the beginning. Just after its explosive origin, the universe consisted of little more than a featureless gas. Now there are galaxies, planets, crystals, clouds, trees and people.

The richness, diversity and variety that characterises the present state of the universe arose only after an extended sequence of physical processes. The story of the universe is one of increasing complexity and organisation emerging spontaneously from primordial simplicity and uniformity. The most striking example of the growth of complexity is in biology, where life on earth has evolved over four billion years from simple single-celled organisms to beings such as ourselves capable of advanced reasoning. Yet it turns out that in order to permit such evolution, the laws of physics need to have a very special form. For example, if the various fundamental forces of nature, such as gravitation and electromagnetism, had differed even slightly from their observed strengths, it is doubtful if life of any sort would have been possible. The apparently contrived nature of the laws of physics was described by the British astronomer Fred Hoyle as "a put-up job". Admittedly, most scientists are reluctant to conclude that these felicitous laws have been deliberately designed by a deity for the purpose of bringing forth conscious life. They prefer to invoke the cosmic selection theory I described earlier.

Nevertheless, the gradual emergence of life and consciousness through natural processes is deeply impressive – far more impressive than a miracle-working deity who simply conjures them into being one by one.

For three hundred years science has been regarded as a dehumanising activity. Its reductionistic and materialistic world view has painted a bleak picture of a universe without meaning or purpose, and of human beings as trivial by-products of nature. Today that interpretation of science is changing. Advances in physics, astronomy and biology are revealing a universe of stunning beauty and harmony in which conscious life plays an integral part.

The rational basis for this ingeniously ordered universe of ours can simply be taken as given, without further enquiry. Or it can be seen as a manifestation of something deeper and more significant. Science cannot prove or disprove the existence of a deeper meaning, it can only offer circumstantial evidence. Each of us must decide for ourselves. The Sea of Faith Network, with its bold agenda for advancing theological thought, and willingness to tackle fundamental issues in a spirit of openness, is well placed to take on board the discoveries of science and the conceptual revolutions that are accompanying them. Science can never provide a substitute for religion, but by incorporating spirituality within an honest scientific framework, the real spiritual needs of human beings can be reconciled with the tenets of our scientific age.

WONDERING PRIVATELY AMONG FRIENDS

Michael Elliott

The Church of England Newspaper of October 22, 1999, carried an article under the banner headline "Bishop Says Keep Doubt out of Pulpit". The item reported an Anglican bishop's admonition, originally published in his diocesan newsletter, advising his clergy that controversial ideas about religion were not to be discussed in the pulpit, but should be reserved for less formal occasions. "There is wide scope", he wrote, "for raising speculative questions in study and discussion groups; and there is, of course, no limit to what anyone may think or wonder privately and among friends." The bishop went on to argue that if licensed clergy are overtaken by doubt, they should withdraw from their ministry. He is clearly not a person who warms to Tennyson's words from *In Memoriam*, "There lives more faith in honest doubt, believe me, than in half the creeds".

The writer of the article, the Archbishop of Canterbury's son Andrew Carey, noted that the bishop's call for speculative theological opinions to be kept out of pulpits was "a move which will be seen as a sharp rebuke to groups like the Sea of Faith and infamous Anglican bishops who question even the most fundamental doctrines of the church". He repeated the bishop's comment that most people "expect authorised preachers and teachers to be faithful to the traditions of Anglican orthodoxy". Rebukes of this order are not altogether bad news for members of the Sea of Faith, if we accept the implication that the Network is a place where people with religious doubts, denied access to the pulpit, can express them in a free, open and supportive environment.

The item was not regarded as newsworthy by the rest of the church press, and perhaps should be read in the context of the Church of England Newspaper's evangelical association prompting its current championing of an anti-liberal crusade. This campaign, which has descended to a level of personal viciousness not seen previously in the church press, is itself a reflection of the major realignment in the Church of England since the Lambeth Conference of 1998. There, some of the evangelical bishops of the South orchestrated a campaign to force the church to abandon its traditional stance of open enquiry based on the principles of scripture, reason and tradition in favour of imposing strict biblical standards of authority and morality.

Characteristically, institutions that are under challenge adopt a siege mentality and resist change in the mistaken view that acting in this way will ensure survival. It seems incredible to free-thinking people, in an era in which scholars have developed exciting new tools of historical and biblical criticism, and where the analytic tools derived from the social sciences have enabled us to understand more about the social, political, cultural and ideological contexts in which texts were produced, that the calling into question of traditional thinking on religion, or any other subject, should be banned from the arena of public preaching and relegated to "private wondering amongst friends".

While the general context of the English bishop's remarks is an affirmation of the "back to basics" call of some African and Asian bishops, at a deeper level they are reinforcing a particular view of education which conceives the mandate of the teacher or preacher as authoritatively communicating a divinely inspired and received truth.

The sociologist Paul Goodman, writing in the 1970s, coined the phrase "compulsory miseducation" to describe the condition of prescriptive education in an unfree society. Many in my generation became unhappy products of curriculum-driven education. Some of us suffered the additional damage of being educated in a setting where the instrument for enforcing student conformity was institutionalised violence, justified by the all-hallowing voice of "tradition". This violence took the form of corporal punishment often randomly administered by the staff, and ritualised bullying in the playground and on the playing field, directed always at those who were the weakest, the most vulnerable, or the recognisably "different" in the community.

When education is viewed primarily as preserving the traditions of the past, it damages human potential for the future. Much of the intellectual and spiritual formation promoted by theological college or seminary training was cast in this mould. In most cases the physical violence ceased, often to be replaced by bizarre acts of self-mortification to encourage an ascetic spirituality, but there persisted in various forms the idea that the student must conform to an ideal derived from the past – in this case, the monastic ideal. In this context of religious formation, the violation of the human personality continued but assumed more subtle forms, and was frequently institutionalised through the discouragement of individual difference, intuition and creativity, which were dismissed as sins of pride or self-seeking. Many prospective Christian ministers were educated into the belief that the individual's needs and gifts must be subordinated to the common good of the religious community.

It takes many years to overcome the damage caused by these church- and state-inspired parodies of education. Speaking personally, one moment of enlightenment came when, as a young priest responsible for education in an extensive suburban parish, I went out of interest to a lecture by a noted authority in child development. At the end of the presentation, one questioner asked how and when one should begin disabusing children about their make-believe worlds. The speaker responded that when a child comes indoors claiming to have seen fairies at the bottom of the garden, the "problem" lies not with the child's perception, but with the adult's lack of perception. For most adults the world has indeed become "disenchanted" and adults themselves disabled, in that education has stripped them of the ability to "read" the world as anything other than a realm of pragmatic concerns.

This "disenchantment of the world" is a phrase that Weber coined to indicate the disappearance of magic as a salvific instrument in human experience. But as the French scholar Marcel Gauchet argued, the term needs to be broadened to embrace "the impoverishment of the reign of the invisible". Paradoxically, Gauchet regards religion itself as the main culprit for this impoverishment, in that religion, turning its back on a natural world in which there was no distinction between the material and the spiritual, deliberately reconstructed the human abode separate from the divine. Later, in the Enlightenment, the pre-eminence given to reason would broaden the rupture between the world viewed as a unity within which passion, intuition, mystery and a sense of the transcendent contributed to what we might broadly call education, and the world falling increasingly under the spell of rationality, scientific certainty and the application of technology. As Rorty describes the approach: "Once such obstacles as the passions or sin are overcome, the natural light of reason will guide us to the truth" (Rorty 1999:114).

We can make a clear distinction, then, between forms of education that are negating of the human spirit of enquiry and those that are affirming of it. At the root of the debate is not simply the question of freedom, as Richard Rorty and Marcel Gauchet both attest, but the way in which humanity regards its past and its future. This in turn directly affects a society's attitude to education. If it looks primarily to the past, it may adopt an apprenticeship model of education in which "The ideal was to gradually internalise and immerse oneself in the knowledge established by one's predecessors so as to honourably step into their shoes and in turn pass on the tradition" (Gauchet 1997:180). A society looking to the future, however, will focus on the formation of the individual, and the appropriate preparation for making a creative contribution to existence.

John Hull, in his provocative book *What Prevents Christian Adults from Learning?*, suggested that one of the problems is that religions like Christianity tend to present a concept of God as all-knowing and that this quality of omniscience encourages people to accept the authority both of God and God's agents. Rarely does religion talk about a learning God or a learning Christ. According to Hull it is this view of "an unlearning Christ who is the image and incarnation of an unlearning God, and is the model and pattern for the unlearning believer" (Hull 1985:201) which has a permanently retarding effect on adult religious learning. In religious systems like Christianity, most members are cast in the role of passive learners rather than teachers; most are regarded as too inadequate or incompetent to "teach the faith"; most are advised to be taught rather than to enquire; and most are encouraged to accept the view that the higher up a person moves in the religious hierarchy, the less they have to learn and the more they have to teach.

Hull contends that while there are passages in scripture which portray Christ as possessing a transcendent omniscience with detailed foreknowledge about individual circumstances and an apparent "inability to be surprised or to display curiosity", there are also passages which portray Jesus as an enquirer, a person open to new learnings and insights, and a person willing to dialogue with others, treating them as equals. But that tradition has been largely smothered by a church that produced accounts of the life of Jesus like the Gospel of Thomas, indicating that there was nothing that his teachers could actually teach the infant, child and adolescent Jesus. Later theological treatises, like those of Clement and Anselm, reinforced the tradition that because learning implies imperfection, Jesus must have been an all-knowing teacher, free from ignorance and uncertainty.

There keeps resurfacing in human history, however, a different way of thinking about education, reflecting the Platonic understanding of education as the awakening of the true self. There have always been those who have been critical of the inductive or apprenticeship approach to education. William Godwin, once a non-conformist minister who today is recognised as the founder of British anarchism, was a vociferous critic of the national education system of his day on the grounds that it rested on the vindication of past knowledge rather than the pursuit of the new, it reduced people to the status of being perpetual pupils reliant on receiving instructions, and it was bound to the aspirations of government which is always wanting to convince people of its legitimacy and strengthen its institutions.

All such education Godwin regarded as despotism, with children being educated like parrots, teachers reduced to a state of slavery to the system and behaving as tyrants, school classes being far too large, and the teaching methods based on compulsion rather than persuasion. Many contemporary teachers find resonances with this nineteenth-century critique in today's classroom.

Godwin proposed education of a different order. In the classroom, he said, there should be neither "preceptor nor pupil", each person studying because he desires to study and proceeding "on a plan of his own invention, or which, by adopting, he has made his own". The task of the teacher is to awaken the mind, "to breathe a soul into the, as yet, unformed mass". The aims of education are to "Learn to think, to discriminate, to remember and to enquire". Godwin's primary concern was with the issues of human liberty and the construction of a free society, and he understood that neither could be achieved on the basis of forms of education which inhibit, repress and coerce.

The Brazilian educator, Paulo Freire, developed a similar critique for the twentieth century. Freire, who had pioneered adult literacy programmes in his home country, was, like Godwin, concerned with the concept of freedom, and in particular with the liberation of politically and culturally oppressed people. Like Godwin, Freire drew a distinction between education that is liberating, and education that is domesticating, and his literacy programmes were designed, in addition to teaching peasant communities to read and write, to enable them through the literacy programme to "unmask the reality" of their social, economic, political and cultural oppression.

Freire's contention was that all people possess a degree of knowledge which they have assimilated from their daily experience, their intuitions and other sources. They are in this sense already "experts" in a range of areas of human activity and life. That expertise needs to be respected and heard. Inductive forms of education, which Freire called the "banking" model, with "empty" students making withdrawals of knowledge from "information-filled" teachers, create and consolidate dependency. On the other hand, education viewed as a dialogical process, through which participants act as both teachers and learners, sharing their expertise in a process of mutuality, is supportive and transformative.

Critical analysis is an important element in the Freirean model, with one of the objects of the educational process being the enabling of people to identify the social, political, economic and cultural constructions in which their lives are lived, and empowering them to transform these into constructions which nourish human freedom and development.

The recognition that all our structures and systems are not simply God-given but are humanly constructed is, of course, mirrored by the Sea of Faith position that religious faith is a human creation.

The educational processes espoused by Godwin and Freire, as I argued in my book, *Freedom, Justice and Christian Counter-Culture,* are tools for radically transforming society. They are also consistent with the Sea of Faith's vision for humanity. All of us have suffered at the hands of educational systems, and particularly systems of religious education, which have been both domesticating and disabling. These systems have encouraged us to think of ourselves as empty vessels waiting to be filled with knowledge. They have taught us to be passive learners, reliant on the expertise, knowledge and judgment of others rather than having confidence in our own experiences and intuitions. They have taught us to fear punishment, both physical and metaphysical. They have insisted that Truth be packaged in creeds, dogmas and doctrines. And now they are insisting that our "doubts" should not be paraded in public where they might influence other people, but should be relegated to private conversations with friends.

The Sea of Faith, on the other hand, encourages the public confession and debating of doubt – including the doubts of those who by profession are ministers of religion. It believes that the expression of doubt is not something that needs to be restricted to private conversations but is an essential element in open enquiry through dialogical education. The acceptance of dogmas as true, and the teaching of them as if they were true, without bringing any critical faculties to bear upon them, links primarily to questions of power and control. It is not in the interests of closed systems to have public doubt expressed about them. When doubts are expressed, then power and control actually passes from the institution to the voicer of the doubts. Freire pointed out that one of the subtle ways in which education is used to ensure conformity is the way in which knowledge can be bundled into tidy packages with the bundles often having little apparent relationship to one another. The teacher is in control of which packages should be delivered and what relationship between them, if any, should be identified. Where the relationship is not declared, education becomes mystifying and frequently linked to ideological considerations.

My undergraduate studies in political science provided a good example of this. Our syllabus looked at political theory since the age of Plato and examined the constitutions of a number of contemporary states. It was a quarter of a century later that I became aware that a very important stream of political thought, sometimes referred to as libertarian socialism but more often as anarchism, had brooked no mention in my studies. Why was this so? It may have been that, intellectually and philosophically, my teachers considered anarchism a devalued concept not worth a mention. But it is more likely that their own ideological commitments and the drive to convey the "commonsense" nature of their views removed discussion of this important tradition from the curriculum. The example reveals the power of the teacher, by divulging or withholding knowledge, to shape the pupil's understanding and experience.

I see the Sea of Faith Network as a meeting point for those who are throwing off the shackles of the old educational system and who are committed to discovering truth in community with others. While the Network is certainly a place where one can wonder privately among friends, it is also a very public forum, in which reservations about religious faith as divinely mediated rather than humanly constructed can be very openly promoted and tested. Its hallmarks are the spirit of open enquiry and the trust members place in human experience over against the dogmatic teachings of many institutions.

The Sea of Faith, on the basis of its members' experiences, has always rejected forms of education that are damaging to the human spirit, and embraced those that enhance it. The Network's long-standing interest in appropriate forms of religious education in schools is evidence of precisely that concern. We need to ensure that our educational processes within the Network reflect the dialogical model of learning, that we trust our mutual experience and expertise rather than seek to rely on the mediated wisdom of the expert. To this end, the new educational programme that the Network has embarked upon is called "Sea Change – a programme of education through dialogue". Its purpose is to provide members with an instrument through which they can explore and promote Network concerns in a non-hierarchical, non-authoritarian and non-coercive manner.

A word of warning needs to be sounded as well. A commitment to experience-based learning can often be betrayed by the way in which an organisation conducts itself, and we need to be constantly vigilant to guard against experience giving way to authority. Is the Sea of Faith annual conference, for example, in danger of reverting to the banking model of education? Has the dominant view of education so effectively socialised us that we find it more comfortable to slip back into the role of passive learner listening to a succession of noted scholars expound their theories to us, and responding with our questions? Do we give up too much power and devalue our own experience when we treat our speakers as experts? Are we in danger, perhaps, of replicating the model of the Sunday school or even the church service, being reassured by the authoritative word, receiving a blessing as it were, and returning to our everyday occupations?

It has sometimes been said of the profile of the Sea of Faith constituency that it has taken many of us almost a lifetime to clear our minds and souls of the impediments that education has placed in our voyage of discovery. If there was more adventure and less regimentation in our schools, more emphasis on life skills than work skills in our colleges, a greater focus on enquiry than on examination in our universities, and more expressions of doubt and less dogmatic certainty heard in our pulpits, then perhaps there would be no need for the Network.

But the old approaches die hard, and for the foreseeable future, there will be an important role for the Sea of Faith. I like Don Cupitt's description of us as the new Socrates, possessing no ideology of our own but with the gift of being able to question and expose the ideologically constructed and damaging views of others. That seems to me precisely the strategy that the man Jesus of Nazareth adopted as he set about exposing the ideological control emanating from the Temple, and offered people in its place the power of a liberating idea.

RELIGION AND HUMAN RIGHTS

Patti Whaley

There has been a great wealth of writing on the relationship between human rights and religion in the past few decades. Much of this discussion follows one or two common threads: tracing origins or intimations of human rights in the various religious traditions, and evaluating how different religions conform to the human rights standard, usually in terms of their ethics and philosophy, but also in terms of actual practice. There is often a certain defensiveness in much of this writing, an aura of religions trying to hold their ground, which reflects perhaps a recognition of the ubiquitous moral power of human rights discourse as compared to the growing uncertainty, at least in the western liberal Christian tradition, about the metaphysical basis for the moral claims of religion.

There appears, on the other hand, to be relatively little discussion comparing the philosophy, purposes and values of religion to the philosophy, purposes and values of the human rights system. Occasionally one finds essays such as Robert Traer's argument (in *Faith in Human Rights*) that commitment to human rights involves an act of faith similar to religious faith, or Michael Perry's argument (in *The Idea of Human Rights: Four Enquiries*) that belief in inherent human dignity as the foundation for human rights is *per se* a religious belief; but by and large writers on human rights seem to regard religion itself as of little interest except in so far as it contributes to or conflicts with the achievement of human rights.

The ur-text for human rights is the Universal Declaration of Human Rights, agreed in 1948 by the General Assembly of the United Nations. Its 30 articles enumerate a range of civil and political rights (e.g. the rights to life, to freedom from torture, to freedom of expression) and social, economic and cultural rights (e.g. the rights to marry and have a family, to education, to work and to leisure). Religious leaders were deeply involved in the drafting of the Universal Declaration and have continued to be generous in their statements of support for it. In recent writing, however, there is an uneasy sense that human rights may have taken over the public moral debate to such an extent that religions are losing a voice of their own, or losing the confidence to debate openly about human rights values versus other values. The situation may be compared to the old debate between science and religion, when religion found itself needing to reconstruct its apologia in response to the new, universal, objective language of science.

54

Indeed, some Sea of Faith members gaze somewhat longingly at the world of human rights and social activism, envying it its clear statement of aims and values and its success at giving ordinary people the opportunity to campaign and take practical action in support of those values. Most of us live in a society where the historically predominant church is fading into irrelevance, and we are undecided about whether to revive it, create a new form of religion, or abandon religion altogether in favour of a secular value system such as that described in the Universal Declaration of Human Rights. In these circumstances, a reflection on the relationship between human rights and religion might help us both to strengthen our understanding of the continuing value of religion in the post-realist or humanist context, and to shape a more concrete contribution both to religion and to human rights. I would like to suggest, very briefly, three ways in which Sea of Faith could usefully engage with human rights at both the philosophical and the practical levels.

First, *by sharing ideas and support in the debate about the ways in which both religion and human rights can claim legitimacy and authority in the absence of absolute or metaphysical foundations*. The widespread loss of belief, at least in Western liberal society, in metaphysical foundations and absolute values has affected religious thought and human rights thought in somewhat similar ways, particularly by opening the door to challenges about whether either system is more than simply an expression of personal or cultural preference. The drafters of the 1948 Declaration did not seem overly concerned about the basis for rights, simply asserting in its preamble that "Recognition of the inherent dignity and of the equal and inalienable rights of all members of the human family is the foundation of freedom, justice and peace in the world". In our less confident era, the idea that human beings inherently "possess" dignity or rights has been strongly challenged, most famously by Alasdair MacIntyre's declaration in *After Virtue: A Study in Moral Theory*, that "there are no such rights, and belief in them is one with belief in witches and unicorns ... [E]very attempt to give good reasons for believing that there are such rights has failed" (MacIntyre 1984:69–70). Certain governments, particularly in Asia and Africa, have exploited these challenges in their own arguments against the universality of human rights, asserting that the supposedly universal values are peculiar to the West and that their imposition on the rest of the world is an expression of cultural imperialism.

Human rights philosophers have responded by arguing that the universality of human rights rests not on its absolute foundation, but on its practical effect: it leads to what an increasing number of people recognise as a better life, and does this more effectively than any other form of social morality which we have yet devised. It is not necessary to argue that human rights are true, but only that they are efficacious; they are based not on what human beings inherently are, but on what we aspire to be.

The similarity to the post-realist view of religion should be obvious. Post-realists are concerned with how to retain religious value in the absence of metaphysical or absolute foundations. Although religious post-realists are less concerned with claims to universality than human rights post-realists, they share a need to revalidate their practice on its own merits, absent of any inherent truth. Like the post-realist human rights philosopher, Sea of Faith's task is not to argue whether God is "true" but to explore the ways in which the religious demand, embodied in God, helps us to achieve a better life. Both involve, to a certain extent, a leap of faith as a precondition for commitment rather than as a result of philosophical or empirical demonstration. Thus, for example, Robert Traer's statement that "faith [in human rights] involves trusting in these standards of human dignity, despite the inability to prove to the satisfaction of all others that the standards are true" (Traer 1991:219) is mirrored by Jack Miles' description of post-realist religion as "the felt necessity – somewhat mysterious in itself – to live a moral life even when the grounds of morality cannot be known" (Miles 1997:59). Human rights and post-realist religion both rely heavily on story-telling as a means not only of expressing known values but of exploring new ones. Richard Rorty, for example, argues in *Human Rights, Rationality and Sentimentality* that the protection of human rights is not improved by arguments about whether humans inherently possess the rights enumerated in the various human rights declarations, but by telling stories that evoke our sympathy for those deprived of their rights (Rorty 1993:111–134). Human rights and post-realist religion both see their ideals as something to be achieved primarily in this life, rather than the next, whether that ideal is "a world in which the rights enshrined in the Universal Declaration of Human Rights are enjoyed by all people", as expressed by Amnesty International, or "a world in which every human life is valued as though it was the incarnation" (Bullock 1996:5).

The post-realist view of religion has so far had less success than the pragmatic argument for human rights, for reasons that are not difficult to understand. The Universal Declaration of Human Rights is primarily a statement of values and aspirations relating to human behaviour rather than a statement of metaphysical belief; to the extent that there was an underlying belief in the inherent dignity of humans, this belief was secondary to the purpose that the Declaration attempts to achieve, and that purpose can survive the loss of the implied underlying belief relatively easily. For religion, at least for the monotheistic religions, a more fundamental shift is involved; the loss of a "real" God appears to many traditional believers to remove the very essence that separates religion from the secular world. Nevertheless, the success of the human rights system should give support to Sea of Faith's view that faith and commitment are possible in a humanist, non-foundational context; and human rights philosophers and post-modern theologians can usefully learn from each other how to justify faith and commitment on the basis of values and practice alone.

Second, *by working with the human rights movement in the philosophical and practical defence of religious freedom for all people*. Religious intolerance continues to be a major source of conflict and suffering in the world, both in terms of conflicts between the religions themselves and as an underlying factor in conflicts between ethnic and political groups. As Hans Küng has repeatedly warned, "there will be no peace among nations without peace among the religions". Religious intolerance against specific individuals, as documented by Amnesty International and others, may take the form of persecution for blasphemy, heresy, apostasy and other transgressions of belief; persecution for certain practices such as proselytism or conscientious objection to military service; or denial of equal rights simply by virtue of belonging to a religion or sect that is illegal or unacceptable.

Efforts to improve religious tolerance take different paths depending on whether one takes a human rights approach or a religious approach. Among human rights advocates, religious tolerance is viewed primarily within a legal framework, as a right to be protected by governments regardless of the state of sympathy between the religions themselves. This legal, rights-based approach can "call a truce" between religions and create opportunities for tolerance and dialogue, but cannot by itself resolve the underlying theological sources of intolerance. Among the religions, religious tolerance is usually based on one of two principles: either one's own religion is the only "true" religion, but all persons are entitled to tolerance, respect and freedom in the choice of religion; or all religions are relatively imperfect reflections of a truth which cannot be empirically proven or cannot be directly (i.e. non-metaphorically) expressed. This latter position is closest to the Sea of Faith view, but still retains a belief that absolute truth exists, even if we cannot grasp it.

Sea of Faith obviously has a particular interest in questions of religious tolerance for both principled and practical reasons. In practical terms, Sea of Faith clergy have an immediate interest in questions about the limits of unorthodoxy that can be tolerated within a religion, and whether those limits apply only to membership in a religion or to licences to preach or teach as a representative of the religion. Being denied a paid position as a representative of a religion, as at least one Sea of Faith member has been, need not necessarily be regarded as a human rights violation in itself. It does, however, highlight questions of principle about the relative weight of dogmatic orthodoxy versus other possible indicators of religious faith which are important not only for Sea of Faith members but for religious tolerance generally. Sea of Faith regards dogmatic belief both as humanly created, and therefore contingent, and as secondary to religious expressions of value and ethics. Both attitudes provide a strong base not only for tolerance of other, equally human, religious beliefs but also for active interest in what can be learned from them. This is not to say that Sea of Faith would regard all religions as equally valid or worthwhile, but that all religions are *prima facie* worthy of examination to see how they may teach us to live a better life. The basis for judging a religion, or a particular person or sect or belief within a religion, is not by the orthodoxy of its dogma but by its success in fostering a sense of meaning, harmony, justice and compassion, both among its adherents and towards those outside its own circle. A stronger involvement by Sea of Faith in advocacy of religious freedom would therefore serve multiple aims: it would provide a means of exploring and promoting religious faith as a human creation, and the theological implications of that mission for religious tolerance; it would provide a broader framework within which our own members could wrestle with their questions about the nature of orthodoxy and the limits which a religion may rightfully impose on its adherents; and it would provide us with a practical way of applying our values in the world. This could be done through supporting theologians outside Sea of Faith who are sanctioned because of perceived unorthodoxy, such as the Sri Lankan Catholic priest Tissa Balasuriya; or through more active alliance with organisations such as the International Association for Religious Freedom and other advocates of religious tolerance and interfaith dialogue.

Third, *by focusing on religion as an expression of values, rather than metaphysical dogma, and rebalancing the debate between religious values and human rights values.* In the same way that human rights has provided an excellent framework for re-assessing religions, there needs to be a religious framework for re-assessing human rights values. The human rights model has become so pervasive and powerful that discussions of differences between human rights values and religious values tend to be phrased as if we assume that the religious "deviations" need somehow to "be reconciled with" the human rights framework; whereas a more healthy approach might be to see the two in a balanced and creative tension, each acting as a corrective to the other. I can suggest only a few examples here, which need to be worked out in far greater detail. I would also note that the values referred to are not exclusive to religious communities; many of them have carried over into secular humanist communities as well. Nevertheless, they tend to be put forward most systematically within a religious context.

Religions tend to value responsibilities at least as much as, if not more than, rights. While human rights communities certainly recognise responsibilities, they tend to view them in quite restricted contexts. For example, in the dialogue between religion and human rights, responsibilities or duties are often described as if they are precursors to rights. The implied assumption is that responsibilities are the way that religions used to state rights before a proper vocabulary of rights was developed, but that this older style of expression has now been superseded by the new rights-based vocabulary. In broader human rights advocacy, responsibility is usually viewed in terms of ensuring the rights of others, a responsibility falling primarily to governments and only recently and secondarily to other parts of society. Little if anything is said about responsibilities which are inherent in and inseparable from the exercise of rights themselves, and attempts to define social and individual responsibilities, such as the 1997 draft "Declaration of Human Responsibilities" advocated by Helmut Schmidt, Malcolm Fraser and others, are viewed with alarm by human rights advocates.

To some extent their alarm is understandable. The risk in trying to counterbalance rights and responsibilities is that a failure of responsibility by the rights-bearer could be taken as a reason for denying a right; i.e., one has "forfeited one's right" to something by virtue of not fulfilling a corresponding responsibility or duty – an argument often used to justify the death penalty, for example. Certainly this would be an unacceptable distortion of the proper balance between rights and responsibilities. But the other end of the spectrum – viewing responsibilities only in terms of general governmental or social responsibility to ensure that each individual enjoys his or her rights – leaves a vacuum at the centre of individual life and removes the sense of profound personal responsibility and action without which ethical systems are simply wishful thinking. The growth of human rights advocacy itself would not have been possible without the deep sense of moral responsibility of the founders and members of the human rights movement; to a certain extent the human rights movement banks on this inherited moral capital while at the same time viewing an emphasis on responsibility as somewhat threatening to the strength of the rights vocabulary. In the long run, rights and responsibilities must be seen as indivisible; the world in which human rights are enjoyed by all will come about not only by people waiting for governments to bestow rights upon them like manna from heaven, or even by campaigning to demand their rights, but by also assuming the personal moral responsibilities inherent in a rights-bearing society.

Religions tend to see both rights and responsibilities as exercised in community rather than in isolation, whereas the human rights system tends to treat persons as autonomous entities. Although the Declaration refers to community and solidarity (e.g. articles 16, 22–26, 28, 29), these references tend to be rather vague in comparison to the rights regarding liberty and equality, and tend to be largely overlooked in human rights advocacy. Again, the fear on the part of human rights advocates is that an emphasis on community will become a justification for sacrificing the rights of the individual to the harmony of the community, a fear validated by the approach to rights in countries such as China, in the name of nation-building or economic progress, or the United States, where the "rights of society" are invoked to justify the infliction of the death penalty on social offenders. This certainly must be avoided. What is sought instead is, as formulated by the Roman Catholic Church, "the rights of persons in the community, and thus ... neither the rights of the individual over against the community nor the rights of the community over against the individual".

The religious emphasis on the value of community should be particularly sympathetic to Sea of Faith, which, at least in its more post-modernist tendencies, sees the individual not as a discrete entity or a permanent self but as a process or "story" defined only by and in relationship to others. Whether we are discussing rights or religious values, we can possess them only to the extent that they have been created within a community and are validated and given meaning by the community. As an individual, one must of course make up one's own mind about one's religious values, rights, or other moral positions; but to try to do so in isolation from a community would be difficult, if not dangerous or even impossible.

Religions tend to value forgiveness and reconciliation as much as justice and accountability. The human rights movement has lobbied strongly for improved accountability for those who commit human rights violations, as a means of establishing the unacceptability of such violations and therefore helping to prevent further violations. This has been extremely important work, which is finally bearing fruit in the establishment of the International Criminal Court, the special tribunals on former Yugoslavia and Rwanda, and recognition in individual countries of their responsibilities to support universal jurisdiction for persons who have committed crimes against humanity. Again without seeking to weaken this trend towards improved accountability, it is important that counterbalancing values of forgiveness and reconciliation also be recognised and that means of realising them in practice be pursued, in order that communities can be healed and rebuilt. The exercise of forgiveness and reconciliation is not to be viewed as an alternative to accountability, but a necessary partner to it.

The attitude amongst human rights advocates to these and similar values seems ambiguous. On the one hand, as noted earlier, individual responsibility and service to a broader community are indispensable preconditions for achieving a true human rights culture. Michael Perry notes the contrast between the "self-regarding" nature of statements of rights as compared with the "passionate other-regarding character" of human rights work in practice. On the other hand, the rights as stated in the Declaration tend to be treated in a fairly absolutist way, with discussion of counterbalancing responsibilities or values often viewed as an attempt to qualify or undermine human rights. Religious organisations, for their part, seem to fear that assertions of counterbalancing values will be viewed as "out of step" with the prevailing human rights culture, and are often hesitant to risk being seen in that light. What is needed is a more careful discussion of how human rights fit into a broader ethical framework, in which neither the human rights world nor the religious world feels threatened by the other.

In addition to a closer comparison of human rights ethics and religious ethics, it is also essential that we retain a sense of the value of religious belief and practice beyond the purely ethical. Human rights, while increasingly accepted and successful as a system of public ethics, does not pretend to be a system of personal meaning or virtue; and yet it often happens that gross violations of human rights raise deep questions about the meaning and dignity of life which are in themselves essentially religious. One only has to think of Viktor Frankl, who was led by his experience in the concentration camps to create a system of psychology based on the need for meaning; or, in a more directly religious vein, the writings of Frank Chikane, of the South African Student

Christian Movement, on the way that his own experience of torture deepened his sense of faith and mission as a Christian. Religious values can supplement and extend human rights, summon us to transcend our own views, limitations and failures, and give our lives meaning even when human rights seem like a distant and impossible dream. By examining and working more closely with the world of human rights activism and social justice, Sea of Faith can learn how better to achieve the aspirations expressed in the Universal Declaration of Human Rights and, at the same time, throw into relief the continuing need for religious value in our lives, to which our Network is dedicated.

The views expressed in this essay are personal ones and do not necessarily reflect the positions of Amnesty International.

MIXED BATHING IN THE SEA OF FAITH

Richard Holloway

What is life and how are we to live it? Those are the questions that come to us with life itself. When we arrive on earth we do not come with an explanatory leaflet attached; we find ourselves thrown into life and we have to figure it out for ourselves. We are getting on with it all the time and only in retrospect does it begin to make some kind of sense to us, and some kind of pattern begins to emerge. That is easier to understand when applied to a single human life, but we also ought to understand it in relation to the life of the universe itself. The astounding thing about the universe is that it was going on and on, living itself forward for billions of years before the capacity for understanding itself emerged in us. Getting your head round that strange fact is disorienting, but liberating. If we accept that it is mind that discovers meaning, it would seem to follow that there was no meaning till we came along to mean it. Even if we believe in the great Mind outside the system we call God, it could not have been known about, either, till we came along to recognise it or posit it. Only gradually does life make sense; and even when or if it does begin to make sense, it is always in the backward look, the review, the summary of the story so far.

One of the interesting twists in all of this is that in the active living forward of our life we inherit stories that offer explanations of its meaning. These stories of meaning are found everywhere, and one recipe for a happy life is to take one of them and make it our own story, internalise it and live by it. Religious stories are the oldest method for understanding ourselves, but they too are subject to Kierkegaard's claim that we live forwards and understand backwards; the stories themselves emerged as part of the living we have done; so we have to acknowledge them and the role they have played as part of the perspective of the backward look. The work of understanding ourselves will involve us in revising, re-interpreting or even discarding the stories we have developed as we live our lives.

One of the most basic stories that we developed was the claim that our life derives its meaning from beyond us, from another sphere. Having no memory of the real history of our own evolution and the evolution of the universe, we invented narratives to account for it, because explanation seems to be one of the requirements of consciousness. An account had to be offered, a cause had to be discovered. To that extent we have always been scientists, who were intent on knowing about our world and ourselves. Religious narrative was our best first guess about the meaning of things, and some elements of that guess are abidingly useful, even though we no longer accept it as a factual account.

Religious narratives become more sophisticated with the emergence of creation stories designed to explain the existence of the earth and its creatures, including humanity. These early accounts introduce the idea of purpose or meaning in life; the human story becomes teleological. People who believe in religious revelation, the idea that information that we could not have discovered for ourselves is shown to us directly by God, claim that the idea of an overarching purpose in life is part of divine revelation. Like actors in a play whose parts are written for them, we do not know what our role is until it is explained to us.

The trouble with the revelatory hypothesis is that it unavoidably begs the question it poses. There is no doubt at all that the idea that life has a purpose did emerge in human history. We can either decide that, with our passion for meaning, we read purpose into life and nature as a piece of retrospective interpretation; or we can decide that we received the knowledge by revelation from God. Whatever explanation we accept, there is no way off the fact that the idea itself comes to or through *us*, either from inside out or from outside in. This has been one of Don Cupitt's most powerful insights, and one that his many critics have never been able to destroy. It is a version of the ancient paradox of appearance: is there a world out there independent of our perception of it? Common sense would suggest to most of us that there is; but the fact remains that we can only know that world through our perception of it. It is our mind, the recording device between our ears, which puts us in touch with it and plays it back for us. There is no view from nowhere, as it were, no out-of-our-mind "take" on it that could establish its independent existence apart from our perception of it. To that extent it is accurate to say that it is our mind that calls the world into being for us, along with everything else, including God.

There is no way out of this paradox; all the solutions we offer turn out to be versions of the same old problem. If there is a God and a world out there, we can only know them, understand them, be in touch with them, through the agency of our own perceptions. This promotes in me neither despair at ever being able to get hold of anything, nor the kind of immobilising scepticism that believes nothing is knowable as it is in itself. What it does compel me to accept is the powerful creativity of human consciousness in the act of knowing. And the fact that consciousness emerged out of the chemical soup of the universe makes it all the more amazing. The universe itself, obviously there before us, is just as obviously only called into being by us, because it is our understanding of it that forms it as a universe, a knowable system; and there is no understanding other than our own understanding available to us. The same is true of our knowledge of God. God, obviously there before us, is just as obviously called into being by us. It is our understanding that has made God knowable, and there is no understanding of God available to us other than our own understanding.

Disorienting at first, to accept the centrality of our own role in the creation of God and the universe is liberating. It lifts us out of the endless contention of trying to prove the unprovable, of insisting that we can be in touch with the reality of things as they are in themselves by some means other than our own perception of them. Even if we insist, perhaps for the sake of our own sanity, on positing the independent reality of what is outside us, such as God and the universe, there is no way to know those things other than the only way we know anything – through our consciousness, our understanding, our perception, the way we add things up. We can't jump out of our cognitive skin and get a view on reality from some other place. Even if we manage to *imagine* such a possibility, how can we get into it except by *ourselves* and *our* consciousness, which is what put us in touch with the possibility itself?

We are stuck here, but it doesn't have to feel like a prison. Whether we believe God is real or a human projection (God could be both, of course), or whether we believe the universe is real or is made up by us (both of which are almost certainly the case), there is no escaping our own creative role whichever way we leap. The stories all come from us, and whether there is any beyondness to them not of our own making is the great unanswerable question.

It is the greatest achievement of the Sea of Faith Network to have brought this insight into the centre of religious discussion in our time. As with many religious leaders, my first reaction to the Sea of Faith was one of anxiety. I was not surprised to read in one of Don Cupitt's books that many believers are afraid to read him. The basis of their fear is worth a moment's exploration.

I am fascinated by the tone of Don Cupitt's recent books. When he began his great work of deconstruction of religious belief over twenty years ago there was an intensity about him that was frightening to many. I have often wondered about the psychology of it all. Was his steadfast refusal to be diverted by pity for frightened believers a ruthless exercise in self-discipline? He loves Nietzsche, and one of Nietzsche's most penetrating criticisms of Christianity is that its ethic of pity weakens people against dealing with the harshness of truth. He called for the kind of tough love that is necessary if we are not to collude with our own delusions.

This psychological approach is not inappropriate in trying to understand the Cupitt project. We know from recent work in the field of human dependency that addicts have to be brutally honest about themselves if they are to overcome the compulsions that imprison them. In a phrase that was current a few years ago, they have to "own" the reality of their condition if they are to become truly free. A more current metaphor comes from the struggle of the homosexual community to emerge from "the closet" and live honestly and openly. Significantly, the language of "coming out" has been used by Cupitt in his most recent books, where his tone is lighter, more playful and affectionate. It is as though the acceptance of his own condition has freed him to love and understand others, particularly those who are still too afraid to face their own imprisonment. Maybe this is why the Sea of Faith has been as much about therapy as theology. It has allowed people from all faith communities to come out of the closets of doubt and admit that they no longer accept the traditional understanding of religion as hard fact rather than as suggestive metaphor and illuminating myth. People who are afraid to read Cupitt are a bit like alcoholics in denial about their true state; they are afraid that if they listen to the good doctor they will have to forswear the drug that consoles them for the loss of meaning in a godless universe.

It is here that the later Cupitt is at his most compassionate and understanding. He understands our need for meaning, but he wants to liberate us from worshipping idols of our own making. In Plato's parable of the cave – another "closet" metaphor – humans are encouraged to move from the world of shadows into the light of reality. The first stage of the journey into light is painful and disorienting, with many temptations to bolt back into the gloom, but we struggle on, because we are meant to live in the real world and cannot be fully human till we do. One of the realities we encounter outside the cave is the multiplicity of narratives of meaning, the sheer variety of the stories we have told to explain ourselves to ourselves. The narratives are themselves fascinating, but they are not as fascinating as their authors, ourselves! I have called this little essay "Mixed Bathing in the Sea of Faith" because one of the best things about the movement is its ability to get us to acknowledge and celebrate the diversity of the human search for meaning.

Even within single religious systems the variety of interpretation of the official narrative has always been enormous, but the plural nature of contemporary culture has made it impossible to be unaware of other systems or stories. This is a highly complex phenomenon, which seems to have been produced by a number of elements. The main one is *globalisation*. We are familiar with this term as a description of the economic system that dominates the world, and we now talk of the global village. But it is a mistake to limit this metaphor to economics. Globalisation has profoundly affected the religious and intellectual currencies in the world. We are now aware of other systems and traditions, other paradigms, using that term to mean "an entire constellation of beliefs, values, techniques that are shared by the members of a particular community", to quote Thomas Kuhn, the originator of paradigm theory. We have got so used to recognising the claims of other value systems that we forget how new it all is. Paradigms or traditions operate at their best when we are completely unaware that we are in one, and we are tempted to claim that our story is not an arbitrary human construct, the way *we* happen to see things, but the way things actually are. Globalisation makes it impossible for us to be unaware of other ways of looking at the world, and it has an inevitably eroding effect on the way in which traditions are held.

The term that is used to describe this process of cultural erosion is *relativism*, and there are two different meanings to the term. One is descriptive: as a matter of fact, it says, your tradition is relative to your context and its inherited perspective. A subtler form of relativism goes on to say that the points of view themselves are all relative, and there is no way in which we can say that any one of them is superior to any other. Whatever we make of that claim, it is important to recognise that one inescapable aspect of living in our kind of society is that we become aware of other cultures and value systems, and that recognition has a relativising effect on them all.

Many people find that living in plural societies induces enormous anxiety in them, because all the landmarks that once guided them have been moved about. One understandable response to this situation is to stick imperviously to one's own tradition and try to impose it on others. Cardinal Thomas Winning, the Catholic Archbishop of Glasgow, who represents one of the most enduring of religious traditions, the Catholic Church, provides a good example of this approach. Catholicism is a system that works with captivating logic, if you accept its founding premise, which is its divine origin and preservation from error. If you are firmly embedded in such a tradition you can provide clear answers to most questions; and you are likely to be baffled by the failure of others to see how obvious they are. It is difficult for absolute systems to live alongside the values of a plural society, which probably accounts for the exasperated voice the cardinal uses in his frequent intrusions into Scottish politics. One of the many ironies of our day is the way religious institutions become expert at taking advantage of rights won for them by the kind of secular societies whose values they publicly scorn. An example of this was the way the cardinal persuaded the new Scottish Parliament to call for the repeal of the Act of Succession, which discriminates against Catholics marrying into the royal family. However, when parliament tried to remove the discrimination against gay and lesbian people represented by Clause 28, he mounted a campaign of opposition. This episode exposes the difficulty felt by adherents of a particular narrative or paradigm of meaning when they find themselves in multicultural societies where no single view prevails and the whole ethos is one that celebrates the virtue of pluralism. The logic of this situation points to the need for a clear understanding of the necessary separation of religion and the state.

The separation of Church and State is an important principle that has been muddled by the history of Britain, with its tradition of national churches. The Reformation settlement, which established particular versions of Christianity in Britain as official, has largely worn out except for a few anachronistic survivals. We should let these go as well, and recognise that churches are voluntary associations that should only have authority over their members, from whom they can require anything they choose to submit themselves to – but that they have no authority over the civil government, which must govern in the interests of all, including the majority who have little or no religion. Cardinal Winning may have a perfect right to deny homosexual rights within the Roman Catholic Church, which people can choose to leave if they want to; he has no right to interfere with the laws and civil rights of Scotland, from which gay and lesbian people cannot abstract themselves. The problem for some religious institutions, both in Christianity and Islam, is that they have memories of times when they called the shots in state as well as in church, so the temptation to try to influence politics in inappropriate ways easily asserts itself. This clearly happened in the campaign against the repeal of Clause 28, as well as the opposition in the House of Lords, abetted by bishops of the Church of England, to the British government's plan to make the age of consent for gay sex the same as for heterosexuals.

These episodes demonstrate the intrinsic intolerance of many of the narratives espoused by particular religious groups. Though they all evolved in a particular context, they assume the universal validity of their prescriptions. The beauty of the Sea of Faith approach is that it celebrates the diversity of the meanings we devise for ourselves in our search for understanding. Because it knows about our weakness for the drug of false certainty, it attaches a health warning to all religious systems. I'll let Voltaire have the last word:

> ... if you have two religions in your land, the two will cut each other's throats; but if you have thirty religions they will dwell in peace.

CAN WE WORSHIP A GOD OF OUR OWN CREATION?

Graham Shaw

I do not think we shall be able to bear much longer the
> dishonesty
Of clinging for comfort to beliefs we do not believe in,
For comfort, and to be comfortably free of the fear
Of diminishing good, as if truth were a convenience.
I think if we do not learn quickly, and learn to teach children
To be good without enchantment, without the help
Of beautiful painted fairy stories pretending to be true,
Then I think it will be too much for us, the dishonesty,
And, armed as we are now, we shall kill everybody,
It will be too much for us, we shall kill everybody.

When I read Stevie Smith in the 1980s I found her perception of Christianity's problems compelling and one of her questions still haunts me:

But must we allow good to be hitched to a lie,
A beautiful cruel lie, a beautiful fairy story,
A beautiful idea, made up in a loving moment?

I accepted then and I still accept many of her terms in defining the debate. When I proposed that "God is not an external reality who imposes himself upon me; instead he is the construction of my imagination and his character reflects my choices" (Shaw 1987:181) I was trying to respond to her call to honesty. There is a moral difference between a fiction that insists on passing itself off as fact, and a fiction that recognises its fictitious character. The one is a lie, the other is a work of art, and the difference is important. Secondly, I learned from Stevie Smith the need to challenge those elements of cruelty which are often implicit in religious beliefs, and which the emphasis on their factual nature frequently disguises. To insist, for instance, on the objectivity of hell relieves those who propagate such a doctrine of any responsibility for its cruelty. That becomes God's problem, not theirs.

I remain, however, much more hopeful than Stevie Smith that Christianity can itself supply the correctives it requires and I think that one of the reasons she lost patience with Christianity was through the disappointment of misplaced expectations. So, for instance, in emphasising that we create the God we worship, I was not suggesting a possible alternative to orthodoxy or pointing to some exciting theological novelty. Much of the unease aroused by the Sea of Faith approach comes from a sense that it has reduced the robust objectivity of traditional faith to a flimsy subjectivity. The fact that we no longer experience such certainty makes us particularly vulnerable to nostalgia for it – and all the disappointment and recrimination implicit in nostalgia. By contrast, the recognition that religious faith has always been a human creation removes the possibility of the very loss that nostalgia laments. Instead it means that in future religion will always be a more self-conscious exercise than it was in the past, but such self-awareness is at least a first step in protecting us from self-deception.

This religious self-awareness is still relatively new, and we have only begun to explore its implications. We are not, of course, the first people to understand religion in this way, but in the past it was only applied to the religions of other people. The Jewish prophets deliberately drew attention to the work of the Gentile idol-maker to discredit the idol. Epicurus and Lucretius saw the priests of religion as exploiting the false beliefs they propagated, but they did not see themselves as priests. By contrast, religious believers have stressed the objectivity of revelation and the reality of God. For religious people to acknowledge that we worship a God who is our own creation is a recent phenomenon and is still widely dismissed as absurd or confused – and, in the case of clergy, as both self-serving and self-deceiving. So Archbishop Habgood could simply dismiss Anthony Freeman as wanting to have his cake and eat it. If such a religious position seems both embarrassing and contradictory, it is perhaps no accident that it has developed primarily in a Christian context, where believers have for centuries dared to affirm that Jesus is both truly God and a real man. In this respect all Christians, even presumably Archbishop Habgood, are used, so to say, to having their cake and eating it. Some indeed might think that such a claim was at the heart of all sacramental religion, in which bread is eaten and the body of Christ conferred.

In the 1990s I resigned my office, but not my orders, in the Church of England and made the decision to ask for membership of the Religious Society of Friends. I am grateful to that Society for allowing me to have what is called "dual membership". That recognises an element of continuing Anglican identity – the friends of a lifetime, the liberal and platonic intellectual tradition that has often in the past found a home within the Church of England, and a devotional tradition embodied in the Book of Common Prayer. What induced a middle-aged Anglican clergyman of conservative sympathies to embrace the Religious Society of Friends? Are Quakers a natural home for those who have come to recognise religious faith as a human creation? I shall argue that if that is so, they also supply an important corrective to the more exaggerated accounts of that position. Just because Quakers are comparatively ready to acknowledge their own religious creativity, it is perhaps easier for them to recognise that the God who is their creation nevertheless has a life of his own.

Anglicans are notoriously eclectic in their intellectual formation, and I am no exception. I first came to the Quakers because of a strand of Anglican thought which is very similar and at times sympathetic to that of Quakers. It stretches from the Cambridge Platonists of the seventeenth century to Dean Inge and Bishop Hensley Henson in the first half of the twentieth century. From John Smith, Benjamin Whichcote and Thomas Traherne, through William Law in the eighteenth century, it represented a coherent outlook that was neither evangelical nor Anglocatholic. Yet it cannot be easily dismissed as liberal in the sense of secularising or modernist. Like the Quakers it represented an English inheritance from the late mediaeval *devotio moderna,* which placed its emphasis on the personal appropriation of Christian belief. Like the Quakers it was largely untouched by the divisive and exclusive claims that have usually surrounded sacramental practice. Like the Quakers it developed a theology of spiritual re-birth, which was very different from the Calvinism that dominated the origins of Anglicanism and still provides the intellectual foundations of its modern evangelical exponents. For me dual membership does justice to the fact that I was brought to the Society of Friends, not so much by their own writing, as by their witnesses within the established church. So while many Anglicans would see their doctrinal commitments as separating them from Quaker insights, in my case there is real continuity. Of course I recognise that I was myself using that tradition to create a particular view of God, but I did not create it out of thin air. I found a tradition to which I responded; but that discovery was also a choice.

In one respect, however, these Anglicans gave me no encouragement to join the Society of Friends. With the exception of William Law they all remained in office in the Church of England, and however subversive their insights, they conformed to the establishment and all were clergy. For many years I had been drawn to a group of religious writers with a much more critical attitude towards Christian institutions and the clerical identity: William Blake, Søren Kierkegaard, Leo Tolstoy, and Simone Weil. These were all alienated figures, and they doubtless exercised a slow alienating influence upon me. They suggested questions that both worried and fascinated me. Why were the consequences of religious observance often so contrary to the promises of religion? How had a religion of grace and forgiveness acquired such a sour and judgmental flavour? Cumulatively they made me acutely sensitive to the relationship between the ambitions of religious authority and the betrayal of grace. None of these writers is compulsory reading for Anglican clergy. I might have preferred to ignore them by remaining complacently ignorant of them. Instead I chose to immerse myself in them, and in so doing was exercising my religious creativity. An unsympathetic critic might observe that a maverick theologian gravitates naturally to such individualistic and eccentric figures. Without their example I would probably not have found either the language or the courage to resist the pressures of religious conformity; indeed I might not have perceived them. There was, however, nothing of playful post-modernism about this, just as none of them would have resorted to the relativist's slick cliché – "I just happen to believe..." Instead, if they demonstrated a path of passionate disengagement, it was for the sake of truth, and their disengagement was itself an almost desperate attempt to communicate.

At this point I want to return to the question of whether Quakers provide a natural home for those who have come to recognise religious faith as a human creation. Certainly Don Cupitt has repeatedly held up the Quakers as a possible model, but that appears to be more a matter of praise than of practice. It is also true that the Sea of Faith Network has attracted a disproportionately large following among Quakers. At first sight that is surprising. Even its strongest advocates would admit that the Sea of Faith represents quite a sophisticated theological position, which has its origin in the disillusionment of a group of Anglican academic clergy. When one recalls the extreme hostility of early Quakers to a learned clergy, one might guess that they would have seen the Sea of Faith as confirming their worst suspicions of academic theologians. At one level it can of course be understood as an illustration of the changing sociological profile of both Anglicans and Quakers at the end of the twentieth century. Religious communities which once exemplified the class tensions between land-holding and commerce have today found a new unity in the growth of the teaching and caring professions. It is also the case that following the Manchester Conference in the late nineteenth century, British Quakers were more thoroughly converted to a liberal theological outlook than any other conservative Protestant body.

There are, however, deeper resonances in the Quaker tradition, which may make it uniquely friendly to a recognition that religious faith is a human creation. The controversies of the seventeenth century were very different from our own, and I doubt whether Quakers either of that generation or this would have much time for nice debates about the finer points of religious non-realism; nevertheless in some respects their theological radicalism anticipates a more modern agenda. That is seen most clearly in the refusal to objectify their insights in terms of the historic creeds and their even more extraordinary treatment of scripture. In a religious world where the final authority of scripture provided the objective reference for all religious controversy, the Quaker insistence on the primacy of the inward testimony of the Spirit was as shocking and destructive to the conventional religious sensibility of the seventeenth century as some utterances from the Sea of Faith are today. His Quaker contemporaries may have been embarrassed by James Nayler, and for various reasons wished to dissociate themselves from him, but his condemnation and punishment for blasphemy represented the orthodox verdict on the whole Quaker position.

Two features in the continuing Quaker tradition are not easy to accommodate to the outlook of the Sea of Faith. In all early Quaker teaching there is an insistence that the Spirit of God is not simply a natural human capacity, indeed it is in appealing to the Spirit of God rather than to human reason that they most sharply differentiated themselves from Ranters. Repeatedly Barclay stressed the objectivity of the Spirit, so that he could speak of "inward objective manifestations in the heart". I would not myself use such language, but against the Ranters and their modern successors I would defend the need to continue speaking of God. The recognition that we create the God we worship does not simply reduce theology to autobiography.

Closely allied to this differentiation of the Spirit of God from human reason is an insistence upon truth. There may be some Quakers today who would simply regard Quakerism as an option for those who like it – it suits some people – but from the time of the first Publishers of Truth most Quakers have been committed to a rhetoric of truth derived ultimately from St John's Gospel. Indeed the two conceptions of Spirit and Truth are complementary and are derived from the Johannine texts that dominated and perhaps inspired the whole Quaker phenomenon. "God is a Spirit: and they that worship him must worship him in spirit and in truth" (4:24) and "When the Spirit of truth is come, he will guide you into all truth" (16:13). Truth in this understanding is not something simply to be possessed and defended; it cannot be taken for granted.

Quakers insisted that truth requires truthful speaking, but that is only one of its aspects; in some respects they seem to have anticipated the existentialist notion of authenticity, but their position is probably best understood in terms of the Platonic assumptions that underlie the Johannine Gospel. As only the good person can know the good, so only the honest person can know the truth. Truth is not therefore to be reduced to a claim about statements; it indicates a personal disposition. This disposition has its own dynamic, a process of spiritual learning, but it is neither relativist nor pluralist. Instead it is profoundly hopeful about the possibility of attaining truth and communicating it. Such truth is seen as God-given, and that conviction underlies the Quaker insistence on testing concerns within the meeting, or indeed holding Meetings for Clearness.

In my own case I did not seek out the Religious Society of Friends simply as a safe haven where my form of theological deviancy might be tolerated. I appreciated their radically personal appropriation of religious belief; when I wrote of a God who lives in the hearts of those who pray to him I hoped that they might recognise such a God as their own – but then I also harbour such hopes of my fellow Anglicans. What drew me to the Quakers was their commitment to truth and the quality of their engagement with it. Sadly I found myself asking whether the Church of England was any longer a place where truth could find a home. I began to doubt whether it represented a community with any respect for or interest in truth. Did it enable people to speak the truth? Did it foster the freedom to explore the truth or the grace to admit mistake?

Three incidents in the 1990s shaped my perceptions. During the debate on ordaining women to the priesthood, I came to realise that the Church of England found it very difficult to engage truthfully with its own past. There was, for instance, little acknowledgement of the passion with which Anglicans had once denounced the public contribution of women to Quaker worship, or that such women's ministry in England was actually older than the 1662 prayer book. Instead, the issue was presented as an entirely modern challenge to which past precedents were irrelevant. At another level, the same lack of historical awareness made it difficult to perceive any fundamental incompatibility between the Enlightenment values that underlie modern feminism and the ancient symbolic hierarchy of holy orders. Instead, a radical course of action was commended in the name of the tradition it was subverting. It seemed to me that the Church of England was in an unhealthy state of denial. Secondly, the appointment of Michael Turnbull to the See of Durham, despite a long buried police record of a prosecution for gross indecency, only highlighted the inconsistencies in Anglican attitudes to homosexuality. In the ensuing controversy the most disturbing note to emerge was the apparent lack of interest among the church authorities in being truthful. The shock was acknowledged, the reality of repentance affirmed, but none of those responsible seemed to realise that moral and religious credibility might be dependent on speaking the truth. Thirdly, there was the episcopal disciplining of Anthony Freeman after the publication of *God in Us*. I was not particularly concerned that the bishops should oppose Anthony Freeman's views, even if some of them were very close to my own. For me the scandal lay in the means by which the bishops chose to defend the faith. Cathedrals and silver plate can easily be guarded by the use of law and a minimum of coercion. Faith, however, is very different, and is usually defended by being studied and practised and on occasion suffered for. In every other field of human inquiry, disturbing theories are dealt with by reason and persuasion, and truth is best served by free debate and speculation. To use the kind of sanctions to which the bishops resorted in Mr Freeman's case must inhibit any honest debate within the church about the fundamentals of theology.

I recall these incidents for two reasons. First, because they led me to ask what were for me new questions about the Church of England. Why does that church find it so difficult to speak the truth about its own past? Why does it feel no need to speak truthfully about sexuality? Why does it find such difficulty in tolerating honest debate about God? Moreover, in each case the first response to the possibility of embarrassing truth has been coercive, seeking to marginalise or expel, rather than to listen or learn. Reluctantly I came to conclude that there was something about the structures of the Church of England, with its combination of feudal prelacy, discriminatory orders, and legal establishment, which actually promotes dishonesty and perpetuates a false understanding of itself and its relation to society. What drew me to the Society of Friends was that the concern for truth had led them to develop structures that were conducive to elucidating it. In their willingness to face the anomalies of their past, their candour in addressing the problems surrounding Christian sexual teaching and their readiness to foster genuine religious debate and live through deep theological differences, I found a striking contrast with the Church of England. Rather than cling to apostolic claims to authority, Quakers have chosen a path of discipleship, and learning demands a willingness to accept that you may have been mistaken.

The second reason why I have recalled those events of the 1990s is that they serve to qualify any romantic tendency to exaggerate the role of the will, which the recognition that we create the God we worship might otherwise imply. Any student of Isaiah Berlin will quickly recognise in the Sea of Faith only the latest offspring of "... romanticism, and in particular the doctrine that forms its heart, namely, that morality is moulded by the will and that ends are created not discovered" (Berlin 1990:237). One of the surprising characteristics of the Sea of Faith Network is how isolated from most other streams of theology it has remained. It has taken the insight of a critical outsider to point out, for instance, how much Don Cupitt and John Millbank have in common (Markham 1998:64f.). Equally, members of the Sea of Faith have been very ready to see themselves as riding the crest of an exciting post-modernist wave, but they have been less receptive to acknowledging their roots in German romanticism. I believe that Isaiah Berlin offers a valuable perspective on its intellectual origins, and it is disconcerting to discover in one of his essays from the 1960s a description of the outcome of romanticism that provides a striking anticipation of the theology of the 1980s:

> The freedom which for existentialists, as for the romantics, distinguishes men from objects in nature consists precisely in commitment to this or that course of action, this or that form of life, which cannot be justified outside themselves. It is mere cowardice – an attempt to take oneself or others in – to look for an alibi outside the human will in some external authority: natural, historical, social, moral. Moreover, it is a contradiction in terms. Authority, justification, purpose – these are concepts which arise only in the course of decisions by individuals to live or act in this or that way; the transference of them to external agencies, divine or natural, can spring only from weakness, fear of admitting that we, and we alone, are responsible for what we do in the area allotted to us, for which we can give no reason save that that is what we aim at, that these are the goals that are ours because we have chosen them – for there is, and can be, nothing else that we can appeal to – only, as Benjamin Constant once observed, the echo of our own prayers, wishes, laments, that come back to us from the brazen dome of an impersonal world as if they were voices from without. (Berlin 1996:190f.)

But Berlin also provides a salutary insight as to its ultimate significance. If he is correct, we should not perhaps expect any more of the Sea of Faith than of the other romantic theologies that have preceded it. He does not underestimate the impact of romanticism: "Profound, transforming, but not decisive" (*ibid.*:191). The situation he describes is one which liberal Christians will quickly recognise:

> We are heirs to two traditions. The later of these has to a degree sub-verted the older; with the consequence that in the face of those who stubbornly continue the older tradition, whether in the shape of Marxism, for example, or of the Roman Church, those who do not accept such doctrines complain of too much moral indifference to suffering caused by men to one another, too ruthless an objectivity. The majority of the civilised members of Western societies continue in attitudes that cause more logical than moral discomfort: we shift uneasily from one foot to another. (*Ibid.*:193)

"We shift uneasily from one foot to another." For me that means that while I recognise that the religious imagination is creative, I would quick-ly move to qualify that statement. It does not mean, for instance, that the religious imagination is arbitrary or that it operates in a vacuum. I must take responsibility for developing an understanding of God that relates the guidance of the Spirit to the search for truth. Such a God is an implied criticism of those views of the divine that equate faith with improbable claims held with fragile, but obstinate, conviction. Faith on this understanding looks to a truth which at the moment still transcends us, but which is never regarded as finally unattainable. It requires in the present a scrupulous truthfulness in what we say and a willingness to learn, which implies that we cannot assume that we possess the truth already. I am very conscious that such a God represents choices I have made during a lifetime, but those choices are only intelligible in the con-text in which they were made and I did not engineer that context. That is why I have tried to indicate as truthfully as I can something of that process, both in terms of my own decision-making and the specific events in which I was involved and to which I was responding. We can-not evade responsibility for our decisions by simply attributing them to God. I would not therefore claim that God made me a Quaker, but equal-ly I doubt if I would have come to that decision without him.

If you had told me thirty years ago that in my fifties I would be Clerk to a Quaker Meeting I would have laughed in disbelief. As a religious per-son, reflecting on my life and its changes, I have tried both to remem-ber and to understand my own decisions, but I would not want to over-estimate the part they have played in giving shape to my life. Honesty compels me to recognise something else that has also brought me to where I am. If I find the language of confession appropriate, and try to trace the guidance of God, it is not I hope simply to legitimate that process, but to do justice to it, not least the curious mixture of happiness and horror with which I view the outcome. At the very least God informs the choices that we make about him, but if our habits and attitudes have constructed him, our creation has a life of its own. Like other human creations, God has his own integrity, which we have to learn to respect. We cannot simply manipulate him to serve our own agenda. I would, however, want to go beyond that minimalist position, and attribute to God the whole context in which our decisions and choices are made. In the continuous questioning of prayer, we learn to distinguish the context, which precedes our being and defines our possibilities, from those comparatively small and always limited areas where we enjoy real freedom. The conviction that we can make a difference is part of the human experience of divine grace. It delivers us from fatalism and despair, but it should not encourage us to overestimate our powers. I am only able to achieve responsibility because I can distinguish between my actions and their context. In this solitary game of spiritual patience God is known in both the rules of the game and the fall of the cards, and only in that context can I play. If God is my creation, so equally I am his, and to make the first point without recognising the second is not only reductive, it is profoundly misleading. As Christians have always recognised in the person of our Redeemer, the divine and the human belong together.

The fashion for post-modernist attitudes has meant that the Sea of Faith often seems to attract people who wish to destroy the rigid metaphysical objectivity of traditional orthodoxy which refuses to acknowledge its own creative work in the theological enterprise, only to replace it with an equally exaggerated account, in which the doctrine of creation *ex nihilo* is simply transferred from the divine to the human agent. I would suggest that talk of a personal God and the personal language of human responsibility are correlative terms illuminating and sustaining each other. In learning to attribute that for which we are not responsible to God, we learn to negotiate our lives in a way that is appropriate to us as personal beings. Such a reference does not put our decisions beyond question, but it helps to form those decisions by directing our attention to the context in which they are made. Those who look to the worship of God to escape their own responsibility, to access a superior power for their own purposes, or simply to abase themselves, will be disappointed by this account, which gives no comfort to such sado-masochistic dramas. Instead the worship of God gives us a sense of perspective so that in attending to him we also discover ourselves anew. In acknowledging that our God is our creation we are forced to confront and to respect our own creativity and freedom. In recognising that we are also his creation, we achieve a sense of proportion, which reminds us that our limitations also supply our definition. Our most intimate identity is not simply an exercise of heroic decision, it is also experienced as a gift, as something that – as we say – is "given".

It may be that only a Quaker perspective allows one to grasp both these insights and forms a worshipping environment where both can be credibly sustained. For Quakers the recognition that we create the God we worship is neither surprising nor threatening, because our practice of worship is so different from most other Christian groups; but the Quaker practice of worship also qualifies that claim, not least in its insistence that worship is what it is about. A Meeting meets to worship, not simply to meet. The word that is spoken in the Meeting is a human word, and yet it is moulded and elicited by the silence from which it emerges, and the silence that follows utterance is itself a test of the appropriateness of what has been said. I find in that fundamental experience of Quaker worship a model that recognises that we create the God we worship but that we would not be who we are without him.

SAVING THE PLANET

Lloyd Geering

As long ago as 1970 the celebrated sociologist of religion, Robert Bellah, discerned the new religious trend as one in which "each individual must work out his own ultimate solutions [in the human quest for meaning] and the most the church can do is provide him a favourable environment for doing so, without imposing on him a prefabricated set of answers" (Bellah, 1970:43–4). This seems clearly to describe the activities of the Sea of Faith Network. Don Cupitt's excellent series of BBC documentaries on the advent of the modern world helped many to understand why they were no longer comfortable in their traditional church institutions. It is not surprising that Sea of Faith emerged in response. The fact that this loosely organised movement grew rapidly in the UK, New Zealand, and now further afield, shows that it met a widely felt need.

Bellah's comment further explains why Sea of Faith has no distinctive theology or doctrines of its own. It should not attempt to enunciate any, other than affirming that the human quest for meaning and fulfilment is a human activity that people must actively participate in for themselves. The role of Sea of Faith is to encourage and support people in that quest by providing the environment in which people from any religious tradition, or from none, can feel free to explore and give one another mutual support.

The Sea of Faith, in expressing concern about itself and its future, has been asking – Where should it go from here? Should it be trying to plan a bigger and better future for itself? That is the trap into which the institutional church has already fallen, with far too much of its time, energy and resources being taken up with self-preservation. This is understandable – though inexcusable, for in the course of two millennia it has become a very extensive and weighty institution – or, rather, a vast collection of now largely independent institutions. Many of them are suffering from rapid decline yet still believe they are essential for their own sake.

The church has long believed itself to have been divinely founded as the vehicle of human salvation. But at the time of Christian origins the apostles were not concerned with the future of a religious organisation. They were concerned with the future of the world. They showed no interest in building up the church as an institution and, if they had lived to see what happened, they would have been very surprised and perhaps quite shocked at the results. As a Roman Catholic scholar once said, "The first Christians went out proclaiming the coming of the Kingdom of God, but what we got was the church!"

So it is not the future of Sea of Faith we should be concerned with, nor even our own personal future (important though that is to us), but the future of human society and the future of this planet. This is the most urgent issue facing humankind today – and for a variety of reasons.

Christendom (a domain ruled by Christ) no longer exists. Conventional Christianity is already disintegrating. We are coming to the end of the Christian era. We face an unknown and post-Christian future in a context of rapidly changing human culture on a global scale. Oddly enough this fact brings us closer in some respects to the expectations of the apostolic Christianity than to the conventional Christianity we are leaving behind. There is a certain irony in that, for there are those, both in the Sea of Faith and to some extent in the traditional churches, who are distancing themselves from the trappings of traditional religion – just as the first Christians did in their day! They were disengaging themselves from the traditional Jewish religion of the time and rejoicing in their newly won freedom. They were wholly caught up with the future. As they saw it, the days of the old order were nearly over. They confidently looked for the imminent coming of a new order, which they called the Kingdom of God.

But while there are distinct similarities between our situation and that of the first Christians, there are also some radical differences. They expected the new order to be ushered in by the intervening and almighty power of the deity who reigned over the universe. Such a belief, however, is one of the chief reasons why traditional religious forms no longer satisfy us or ring true for us. They were based on that dualistic view of reality that divided it into two – the heavenly and the earthly, the supernatural and the natural, the spiritual and the physical, the divine and the human, the eternal and the temporal.

For an increasing number of people in the modern world, including those in Sea of Faith, the concept of the supernatural has lost the reality it used to have for our forebears. For us the only real world is the natural world, or what we now have come to understand as the vast space – time continuum. All of reality is a unity rather than a duality, even though it resides in a vast and complex universe that is more than our human minds can fully grasp. Moreover, we humans regard ourselves as unities or unified organisms. We may still choose to use such terms as mind, spirit or soul to refer to important aspects of our conscious existence but less and less do we think of ourselves as spiritual entities who are temporarily resident in physical bodies, preparing ourselves for departure to another world. Our individual existence is forever tied to a particular age in the unfolding history of human culture on this planet home, which itself is like a speck of dust in the vast universe.

Although this view of reality has been slowly emerging over a period of some four hundred years, much of the former dualistic view of reality still remains present in traditional religious language and practices, and is thus assumed in the life of the church. There is great reluctance in the church, even amongst many of its biblical and theological scholars, to concede that the Bible is just as human in origin and content as any other book, and that the church, far from being a supernatural society of divine origin, shows itself to be all too human. The church's claim to be a unique channel for divine revelation and, hence, in possession of a unique body of revealed truth, has set it on a collision path with other claimants to truth, such as the whole scientific enterprise, modern historiography and other religious traditions.

The acknowledgment of the Bible as a human book, and of the church as a human organisation, also delivers us from the temptation to idolise. In doing so, by another strange irony, it brings us back to the most basic religious insight on which the Judeo-Christian-Islamic faiths are founded – the rejection of idolatry. We should not worship, or treat as supreme and absolute, *any thing that has been humanly created.* And, since language itself is a human product, all of our concepts, including our concept of God, our doctrines and the Bible, have been humanly created. Thus, as soon as we acknowledge the human origin of religious traditions and of everything within them, we must avoid idolising them. This does not mean, however, that there is no value to be found in religious traditions just because they are of human origin. In Sea of Faith we say we are "free to draw upon our spiritual heritage without being bound by it" – a stance which makes available to us all the rich variety of other traditions and cultures.

In learning to value the totality of human culture and spirituality we also come to realise how dependent we are on our own cultural inheritance. In the past, our spiritual forebears felt themselves to be dependent on the will and activity of God, the supreme supernatural being. For us, that feeling of dependence has been replaced by a feeling of dependence on the countless generations before us who helped to create the culture we inherited. What our forebears once attributed to the creativity of the divine heavenly creator, we must now attribute to our cultural ancestors, and with a similar degree of gratitude. We humans are all products of a particular culture. We can only become human within a living culture. For this we must be grateful. It is salutary to remember that, to the end of our days, we all reflect the culture that has shaped us.

But though we reflect the culture of our birth we are also free, within limits, to reshape it and direct its future. Whenever a particular culture, such as that of traditional Christendom, has been seen as supernatural in origin and hence reflecting some absolutes, the human response has consisted chiefly in trying to conform to it and to preserve it. The only change that was acceptable was that which was believed to be ordained by divine or supernatural forces. Any human challenge to what was ordained was strictly forbidden. In actual fact a good deal of creative change did take place even so, but it usually occurred unconsciously. One of the differences between the past and the present is that the release from commitment to absolutes, and the resulting freedom to change and to create quite consciously, requires us to look at the grave responsibilities that rest on us as a result. While our forebears looked to a heavenly supernatural being to order future events, we see that the future lies largely in our own hands.

We are currently entering a new cultural age. It may be called the global age because nothing and no one around the globe can long escape being caught up in radical global change. Through trade, communication networks, faster travel and cultural mixing we humans are being drawn into one common world with the same destiny for us all. There is emerging a new global culture, based on a one-world view of reality. While beliefs of a dualistic and supernatural kind will survive in pockets for quite some time, they will be confined to private personal convictions and will form no part of common discourse within the shared belief system of the global culture. The very existence of Sea of Faith is one small sign, among many others, that we are coming to an end not only of conventional Christianity, but of a whole cultural era, some two thousand years or more in length, in which Buddhism, Christianity and Islam have been the three most widespread cultural traditions.

Like the first Christians, we too are aware of cultural change and are concerned about the future. However, they were able to take comfort in the belief that the future was in the hands of one who had their best interests at heart. The announcement of this, in the context of impending doom, was quite legitimately spoken of as the Good News, and was the substance of the Gospel they proclaimed.

The recognition that the future is largely in our own human hands can bring to us quite mixed and even contrary feelings. It may be greeted with enthusiasm by some and with great alarm by others. At the beginning of the twentieth century there was considerable optimism about the future. Christians, in particular, confidently expected that the whole world would become Christian within a short space of time. Westerners, in general, believed that science and technology were transforming the earth into a kind of Utopia.

At the start of the twenty-first century, a very mixed set of moods prevails. Those who look into the future with great optimism include two quite contrary groups: fundamentalists who believe God will shortly break in and establish his eternal rule; and those who have such confidence in the human species that they believe we humans are clever enough with our science and technology to meet all current and future problems. But an increasing number look into the future with alarm, ranging from a sobering sense of concern to one of deep pessimism. Such people doubt if the human species does have the wisdom to handle the coming nemesis we have brought upon ourselves. Even those who are reasonably positive about the human condition on a purely individual and personal basis often see scant grounds for hope on the planetary scale. The six billion of us currently living on this planet not only have no concerted plan but are mostly much more concerned with what happens to us individually within our own tiny patch. Humankind as a species is being left to blunder along with the same blindness that has apparently marked biological evolution on the planet from the beginning. This being the case, we humans may well go the way of the dinosaurs.

There are two chief spheres in which urgent global planning and decision-making has to take place to ensure a viable future for humankind. The first has to do with international relations. The still rapidly expanding human population is making ever-greater demands on the earth to provide the necessities for life. This promotes competition and national rivalry for ownership and control of the earth's limited resources – which in turn leads to animosity, friction and war. The United Nations organisation, which was created fifty years ago to preserve the world from further world wars, is finding itself to be increasingly powerless and is now due for a radical overhaul. But so jealous are the nations of their own sovereign identity – and this applies particularly to the five permanent members of the Security Council – that they are reluctant to surrender any of their national sovereignty to an international body in the interests of humankind as a whole. Underneath the problem of establishing and preserving peace among the nations is a whole host of complex problems of a social, cultural and economic kind, where questions of justice, anti-social behaviour and the needs of the disadvantaged are often so pressing that the majority of people are prevented from seeing anything beyond their own immediate concerns. For such reasons, self-interest (both at individual and national levels) could prove to be the death-knell of the human species, at the very time when global concerns are assuming gigantic proportions.

The other sphere calling for urgent decision-making concerns the way we humans relate to the planet of which we are a part. It is becoming increasingly clear that our expanding technology is causing changes in the atmosphere and the environment; these changes, small in themselves, could have devastating long-term effects on both human and non-human species. Very responsible people are warning us that we humans face a global crisis no later than the early part of the twenty-first century because of a number of interdependent factors, all of which add up to an alarming picture unless adequately faced. They have to do with such things as pollution of the basic commodities of air and water, depletion of the ozone layer, loss of arable land, deforestation, climate change due to human factors and irreparable damage to the ecosphere.

Another example of religious irony is that the word *salvation*, so long central to the Christian tradition, is today coming into wide use within a secular context. In the first century it was expressed as "What must I do to be saved from the coming judgment of divine wrath which will precede the ushering in of the new order?" Today it takes the form of "What must we do to save the planet from the destruction we are currently bringing upon it?" Saving the planet is now becoming a religious issue – indeed the chief religious issue. It is properly called religious because, to use Paul Tillich's famous phrase, our "ultimate concern" is now the salvation of the planet for the future generations of humankind. This has become a moral imperative of the highest order.

This is the future which takes precedence over all others, and to which all nations, cultures and religions must give their attention. It takes precedence even over our own personal future, precious though that is to us as individuals. It is the future about which the Sea of Faith should be concerned. The human species is about to face the most testing period in its long existence on this planet. Are individuals, nations, cultures, religious traditions prepared to sacrifice various aspects of their own self-interest for the sake of the future of the species? The great spiritual traditions of the past have all made much of the virtues of sacrifice, self-denial, altruism and caring for others. We will need to draw upon these spiritual resources to the full if we are to meet the imminent challenges of the future.

RELIGIOUS BELIEF WITHOUT REPRESENTATIONAL TRUTH

Philip Knight

Most members of the Sea of Faith Network would probably describe themselves as religious pluralists, but would take exception to the reliance which some versions of religious pluralism place on a representational theory of truth. Proponents of a representational theory of truth argue that true beliefs correspond to some intrinsic feature of reality. Many representational religious pluralists argue that religious beliefs directed toward the ultimate source of all genuine religious truth correspond to reality in a way which religious beliefs that remain fixed to the parochial interests of a particular religion's truth-claims do not. However, members of the Sea of Faith Network who have digested a Cupittean theology will be as puzzled by the notion of an "ultimate source of all genuine religious truth" as they are by the claim that the beliefs of one particular religion represent the truth. Rejecting both notions, they will offer instead a non-representational religious pluralism.

One way to get to grips with the difference between representational and non-representational religious pluralism is to note where they differ on the issue of inter-religious dialogue. According to the representational religious pluralist, Leonard Swidler, inter-religious dialogue operates in at least three different but overlapping areas. Non-representational religious pluralists will pursue the first two areas Swidler identifies, but not the third.

In dialogue area 1, Swidler argues, participants address the practical needs of human communities. They seek to put into practice agreed programmes designed to relieve poverty and hunger, improve health care and educational opportunities, combat racism and other forms of intolerance and to create a more co-operative, just, equal and happier society. Participants in dialogue area 1 hope that greater social and economic security will reduce the potential for inter-religious conflict. In dialogue area 2 the main concern is spiritual understanding. Here, dialogue partners are required to communicate their own faith in such a way that they can, with empathy and imagination, understand one another's beliefs. Participants in dialogue area 2 hope that mutual understanding will also reduce the potential for inter-religious conflict. In dialogue area 3, the main concern is a cognitive quest for truth as well as for understanding. Participants in dialogue area 3 hope that a universal theology of religions centred on a shared religious truth will help to achieve the hopes expressed in the other two areas of inter-religious dialogue (Swidler 1987:16–20).

For non-representational religious pluralists, dialogue 3 is superfluous to the agreements and understanding sought in dialogue 1 and dialogue 2 and is responsible for the continued plausibility of both religious dogmatism and metaphysical scepticism. The first section of this chapter offers a brief summary of representational religious pluralism, noting the link it forges between inter-religious dialogue and truth. The second section then summarises the non-representational account of true beliefs offered by the American philosophers, Richard Rorty and Donald Davidson. Their work supports the possibility of a non-representational religious pluralism which values dialogue 1 and dialogue 2 but which dispenses with dialogue 3.

Representational religious pluralism and truth

Representational religious pluralists argue that the historical and cultural relativity of religious beliefs and the role played by the imagination in the religious consciousness mean that it is no longer morally acceptable to assert that one particular religious tradition has privileged access to religious truth. Instead, they argue, each genuine religion should be recognised as one of many symbolic representations of truth. Although each religion is unique "[t]he truth of all of us", writes Wilfred Cantwell Smith, "is part of the truth of each of us" (Smith 1981:103). Partially represented in every genuine religion, truth becomes the common focus of inter-religious dialogue. As Maurice Wiles writes, "it is only if we are prepared to enter into such [inter-religious] dialogue … that we will be in a position to lay claim to a serious concern for truth … [T]ruth", he adds, "is the goal rather than the present possession of every religion" (Wiles 1992:42–43). John Hick argues that genuine religions are reality-centred. That which Hick rather vaguely terms "the Real" is conceived as the true goal of all genuine religious devotion. The Real is neither personal nor impersonal but justifies its various symbolic representations as personal or impersonal depending upon the contingent cultural categories that constitute the conceptual schemes of religious adherents (Hick 1989:10–15, 36–55).

Despite subtle differences, most representational pluralists draw upon this Kantian epistemological model: mysterious ineffable content, intuitively perceived or transcendentally defined, is schematised by the cultural categories available to different religious people and represented variously as "Trinity", "Brahman", "Nirvana", "Allah" and the like. Summarising the function of the pluralists' representational concept of truth, S. J. Samartha writes:

> All existence is rooted and grounded in a mysterious, transcendent Centre, which is the source of all truth and holds all things together in its embrace. This is the Ultimate Mystery, the Truth of the Truth (the *Satyasya Satyam*) which is the fountainhead of all values and the criterion to judge all human efforts in history .... This language is necessary because in a religiously plural world, the Name of this Mystery is expressed in different ways through different symbols and different words. (Samartha 1991:153–4)

The existence of the "truth of the truth", described by Swidler as "an object in the centre of a circle of viewers" (Swidler 1987:11), makes dialogue 3 and a universal theology of religions plausible. According to Swidler, a universal theology of religions demands that Christians and non-Christians alike "seek to recognise the same truths, the same insights, wherever they find them" (*ibid.*:45). With only partial perspectives on the truth, he notes, "we need to engage in dialogue with those who have differing ... religious viewpoints so as to strive toward an ever fuller – but never ending – perception of the truth of the meaning of things" (*ibid.*:12). Like Wiles, Swidler conceives truth as a generally shared religious goal – a goal unknowable in itself but more clearly understood the more religious believers enter into dialogue with each other.

However, it is not clear that the representational pluralists' understanding of the "truth of the truth" is any more able to escape its particular socio-historical locale than are the ultimate claims made by adherents of particular religions. When representational religious pluralists employ words like "ineffable", "mystery", "ultimate" and "the Real" to depict the primary focus of religious devotion, they simply replace traditional historically conditioned terms ("Trinity", "Brahman", "Nirvana", "Allah" etc.) with their own equally contingent contemporary cultural concepts. Rather than providing a neutral site upon which to build a universal theology of religions, these concepts relativise religious beliefs against a philosophical background of the pluralists' own making. As a result, much religious diversity may fall beyond the scope of representational religious pluralism.

The concern is that religious people who fail to accept that their own religious truth is only partial will be considered by representational pluralists as strangers to the community of inter-religious dialogue. Swidler exemplifies this concern when he claims that "only those who understand all truth statements … to be always limited in a variety of ways, and in that sense not absolute, can enter into dialogue" (Swidler 1990:61). Anyone not prepared to accept the pluralists' "truth of the truth" – anyone not prepared to join the circle of viewers and accept that each viewer has only a partial perspective on the truth – will be unable to dialogue appropriately.

Nevertheless, in the interests of mutual security and continuous mutual understanding, it is conceivable that exclusivists among different religious traditions may find common cause with each other and with pluralists, and so willingly participate in dialogue 1 and dialogue 2, while remaining unpersuaded by the demand of dialogue 3 to give up their own truth-claims. Swidler (1987:38–40), though, seems to suggest that dialogue is only for those fortunate few who have reached stage 5 in James Fowler's account of faith development – a stage congruent with the representational pluralist's own religious self-understanding. This implies that fundamentalists and exclusivists in each of the world's major religions, as well as adherents of self-centred cults, witchcraft, paganism, new-age religions, and even some religious humanists, *may* all find themselves excluded by representational religious pluralists from the processes of inter-religious dialogue.

Not only does this neo-religious dogmatism about truth potentially exclude from dialogue more religious people than it includes, it also makes metaphysical scepticism seem plausible. If the goal of dialogue 3 is an unknowable religious truth partially represented "in different ways through different words", there will always be good reason to doubt that any proposed truth-candidate actually represents this truth. It is possible to have some idea of what it means to say that an individual or a community is getting closer to various contingent goals but impossible to have any clear idea of what it means to say that religious people are getting closer to a fuller perception of "the truth of the meaning of things", or that dialogue is the way to strive toward such truth.

Religious dogmatism and metaphysical scepticism are both plausible outcomes of representational religious pluralism. The next section of this chapter argues that the philosophy of Richard Rorty and Donald Davidson supports the development of a non-representational religious pluralism, which dumps the idea that truth is a goal of inter-religious dialogue. This non-representational approach impugns those features of representational religious pluralism that continue to make religious dogmatism and metaphysical scepticism plausible, but shares the representational pluralists' valuation of dialogue 1 and dialogue 2.

A non-representational view of truth and inter-religious dialogue

Richard Rorty is unconvinced by representational theories of truth. They require a speaker to assume a privileged standpoint from which to compare a contingent description of "X" with description-free features of "X". Leaving aside the question of the plausibility of such a standpoint, the very insistence that truth can be represented, Rorty argues, itself runs up against the intractable problem of defining the indefinable. Truth is an absolute concept and an absolute concept cannot be defined in contingent propositions without raising sceptical questions about the ability of the contingent to grasp the absolute – questions which tend to engender dogmatic responses. "This is why", Rorty writes, "the God of orthodox monotheism, for example, remains so tiresomely ineffable" (Rorty 1998:3). It is also why Hick's "the Real" remains so vague and why "the truth of the truth" is conceived as an ultimate mystery.

Truth, Rorty argues, is an absolute and indefinable concept but, he adds, the practical circumstances in which an appeal to truth is made are neither absolute nor indefinable. "Granted that 'true' is an absolute term", he writes, "its conditions of application will always be relative" (*ibid.*:2). These conditions will be relative to a use of language and to the purposes true beliefs serve, but not relative to an ineffable reality. As Rorty (1989:5) succinctly puts it, "where there are no sentences there is no truth". True beliefs, Rorty argues, are contingent linguistic tools fulfilling contingent human needs. They are not representations of something absolute and beyond. "There is", Rorty writes, "a human activity called 'justifying beliefs' that can be studied historically and sociologically but this activity does not have a goal called Truth" (Rorty 1998:163).

In *Philosophy and the Mirror of Nature* Rorty delivers a sustained critique of representationalism. Descartes and his successors, Rorty argues, fashioned historically contingent Greek ocular metaphors such as "the Eye of the soul" into the mind's indubitable representational processes. By explaining true beliefs in terms of mental representations, they made it virtually impossible to give a satisfactory answer to the problem of how a mental representation connects to its material counterpart in the external world – a problem no less intractable when language rather than the mind is understood as the representational medium. Philosophers ever since have proposed various versions of metaphysical realism and idealism in the hope of accounting for the mind-world (or word-world) hook-up, but their starting point of privileged representations only ever averts scepticism at the expense of dogmatism – witness Logical Positivism's unverifiable verification principle. Instead of seeking to explain true beliefs, Rorty argues, Descartes and his successors should have been content to settle for "conversational justification" – the reasons people give for holding beliefs true.

Conversational justification is non-representational. It is, Rorty writes, "a social phenomenon rather than a transaction between 'the knowing subject' and 'reality'" (Rorty 1980:8). As a social phenomenon, language does not create representational *copies* of reality, but an endless variety of ways for *coping* with reality. The linguistic tools that humans have had the luck to evolve, such as beliefs and desires, help people to deal with the environment and are causally related to the environment. However, a Darwinian account of our origins, Rorty argues, can make little sense of a distinction between beliefs that penetrate the veil of appearances to reveal reality, and beliefs that do not. The only distinctions to be drawn are between the different purposes beliefs serve. Some purposes people have are served by holding beliefs about atoms or genes, while other purposes are served by holding beliefs about freedom or the requirement to praise God. These beliefs allow people to *cope* with reality in different ways but they neither represent nor fail to represent something called "the truth of the matter". To claim that they do says a lot about the kind of people who make such claims, but little else.

If the project of adjudicating between beliefs on the basis of some indubitable representation is dumped, truth ascription will no longer carry metaphysical significance. Ascribing truth to one's own religious beliefs will not show that they possess a privileged quality which the religious beliefs of others lack, nor will it affirm a common goal which the religious beliefs of others share. Rather, ascribing truth to one's own religious beliefs will simply show that those beliefs are commended by a particular social audience. In this context, religious dialogue might seek to understand the different religious beliefs and purposes people have – the aim of dialogue 2 – and, as far as is possible, seek agreement between these people – the aim of dialogue 1. However, there is nothing for the would-be participant in dialogue 3 to discuss.

Having dispensed with representations, Rorty sees no need to deny that people regularly affirm beliefs to be either true or false. The adjective "true", he argues, is used by communities of speakers in sentences that endorse, commend, caution and infer beliefs. Endorsing a belief, a speaker might say, "I see that what you told me yesterday about the footballer's skill is *true*". Commending a belief, a speaker might assert, "It is *true* that those dumplings are the best anyone will ever taste". Cautioning against a belief a speaker might warn, "The expectation you have that your car's engine will start tomorrow is perfectly justified but may not be *true*". Inferring a belief, a speaker might reason, "If what the teacher says is *true* then the candidate will pass her exams". However, none of these examples need lead, in Rorty's words, "[to] our nominalising the blameless, indispensable, and unanalysable adjective 'true' into a far-off object called Truth" (Rorty 1998:165). In each case "true" has a practical rather than representational significance. A cautionary use of the word "true", for example, as in the statement "This belief may be justified to your community but still not be true", does not show that a person has two responsibilities, one to the truth and the other to the community to which they justify their beliefs. "[I]t merely shows", Rorty writes, "that what can be justified to some audiences cannot be justified to others" (*ibid*.:27).

To suppose that the phrase "it's true" *explains* why someone should be a Christian rather than a Sikh, or a theist rather than an atheist is, Rorty argues, to confuse the justification of beliefs by other beliefs – i.e. the *reasons* anyone gives for supposing his beliefs true – with the justification of beliefs by non-beliefs. This confusion is an example of what Donald Davidson has called "the third dogma of empiricism", according to which empirical content (things and events), organised by a conceptual scheme, determines the truth of beliefs. Davidson's critique of this scheme–content (mind–world) distinction and his proposal of an alternative "triangular" account of true beliefs supports the non-representational religious pluralists' conception of inter-religious dialogue and has led Don Cupitt to describe himself in *The Last Philosophy* as an "orthodox Davidsonian" (Cupitt 1995:33).

According to Davidson, philosophers who argue that true beliefs are justified by the world have not explained satisfactorily how such justifying activity can free itself from the other beliefs people hold. Justification is propositional and therefore, Davidson notes, "[r]ealism, with its insistence on radically non-epistemic correspondence, asks more of truth than we can understand" (Davidson 1990:309). The world causes people to hold beliefs, Davidson argues, but the truth of those beliefs is not established by a correspondence between beliefs and the world.

Davidson also rejects the idealist's strategy that would reduce the patterns the world makes to the patterns of a mental scheme. This idealist strategy creates the ridiculous possibility that people's beliefs about the same things might vary independently of anyone's immediate contact with the environment. Epistemic (mind-dependent) theories of truth, Davidson suggests, "reduce reality to so much less than we believe there is" (*ibid*.:298–9). Defining truth in terms of meaningful patterns of epistemic coherence gives priority to a conceptual scheme at the expense of the external conditions that regularly cause people to hold beliefs true. Being largely shared, Davidson argues, these conditions – an external environment and an ability to communicate with each other – reduce to nil the possibility that conceptual schemes might comprehend the world in radically different ways. Consequently, the scheme–content distinction serves no purpose. To drop this distinction is also to drop the idea of a third reality – experience, language, sense-data etc. – that mediates between knower and known. If knowing is immediately related to the environment, neither correspondence nor coherence theories of truth have any role to perform.

However, Davidson does see a use for a non-representational concept of truth within a theory of interpretation that identifies the content of people's beliefs. This non-representational concept of truth builds upon the semantic concept of truth offered by the philosopher of logic, Alfred Taski. In Davidson's words, this non-representational use of the concept of truth claims that:

> ... truth for a language L must entail, for every sentence *s* of L, a theorem of the form '*s* is true if and only if *p*' where '*s*' is replaced by a description of *s* and '*p*' by *s* itself if L is English and by a translation of *s* into English if L is not English. (Davidson 1984:194)

Put crudely, if '*s*' is the English sentence "Jack is holding a carrot", the truth of this sentence does not depend upon a *reference* to a real Jack or to an actual carrot, but upon a formal and admittedly tautological *inference* such that: "Jack is holding a carrot" (*s*) is true if and only if Jack is holding a carrot (*p*).

This formal inference ('*s* is true if and only if *p*' – where '*p*' is a restatement of *s*) can be applied to any sentence asserted by a speaker. It allows the attribution of truth to a speaker's beliefs but does not define truth in terms of coherence, correspondence or anything else. It neither provides the interpreter with information about what a speaker knows nor does it posit a word–world relation that makes a speaker's sentences true. An interpreter may be totally unaware of what a speaker from the Netherlands asserts when that speaker says "Jack houdt een wattel", but by applying this formal concept of truth to the Dutch speaker's assertion, the interpreter can know that for the Dutch speaker "Jack houdt een wattel" is true if and only if Jack houdt een wattel. This formal concept of truth links interpreter to speaker without requiring that they share a language in common. However, in order to understand the meaning of a speaker's utterances, and thus the content of a speaker's true beliefs, an interpreter must, in addition to a formal concept of truth, apply to these utterances what Davidson calls the "principle of charity".

The principle of charity, Davidson argues, requires an interpreter to assume that *most* of the beliefs a speaker holds true are true for the speaker, that *most* of these true beliefs are rationally consistent and that the patterns of rational consistency an interpreter applies to her own beliefs also apply to the beliefs of a speaker. The first two of these three assumptions are the unavoidable consequence of having ascribed beliefs to a speaker in the first place. The third assumption, which makes a wide divergence between the beliefs a speaker holds and the beliefs an interpreter holds unlikely, is a consequence of the fact that belief ascription is a matter of interpreting a speaker's words in a shared world of objects and events. Alongside charity and a non-representational concept of truth, it is this third factor – the verbal and other behavioural responses a speaker makes to external objects and events – which furnishes the interpreter with an understanding of the content of a speaker's true beliefs. In the context of interpersonal exchange the interpreter notices, for example, that Jack has hold of a carrot every time the speaker asserts "Jack houdt een wattel" and so comes to understand the content of the Dutch speaker's true belief. Toward the end of his essay "Empirical Content" Davidson explains:

> It is not the *speaker* who must perform the impossible feat of comparing his belief with reality; it is the *interpreter* who must take into account the causal interactions between world and speaker in order to find out what the speaker means, and hence what he believes. (Davidson 1986:332)

Only when the interpreter correlates the *responses* of a speaker to objects and events in the external world of the interpreter, forming a triangle between a world and two points of view, can a speaker's beliefs be understood. This is Davidson's triangular account of true beliefs. Truth, for Davidson, is an indefinable formal concept, which humans require in order to interpret and understand one another. It serves no useful purpose to suppose that truth is also a mental/linguistic representation or a goal of dialogue. Davidson notes:

> Of course, if we have beliefs, we know under what conditions they are true. But I do not think it adds anything to say that truth is a goal, of science or anything else. We do not aim at truth but at honest justification. Truth is not, in my opinion, a norm. (Hahn 1999:461)

The aim of triangulation is to show how interpretation makes understanding possible. Understanding discounts the possibility that people's beliefs might be radically out of touch with each other. However, understanding does not dissolve differences of opinion. "The aim of interpretation", Davidson writes, "is not agreement but understanding" (ibid. 342). Maintaining a distinction between understanding and agreement/disagreement, Davidson hints at a dual role for dialogue. In one role dialogue follows triangulation. "Once we understand each other so that we can have a dialogue", Davidson says, "then we can meaningfully disagree or agree". (Davidson 1994:53) We can only agree/disagree with the proposition "Jack houdt een wattel" if we understand what the speaker means. Elsewhere, however, Davidson indicates that dialogue also coincides with triangulation. "What is created in dialogue", he notes, "is not a common language but understanding". In this latter role, dialogue brings forth understanding by means of triangulation, while in the former role it seeks agreement after triangulation has created understanding.

Applying these two moments of interpersonal encounter to inter-religious dialogue the non-representational religious pluralist will equate dialogue 2 with the ability to triangulate – the ability to interpret and understand different people's religious beliefs and practices. This ability makes both religious agreement and disagreement possible but it cannot guarantee agreement over disagreement. Seeking agreement, the non-representational religious pluralist will require a second-level discourse – dialogue 1. This second-level agreement-seeking discourse will detail goals and procedures by means of which interested parties endeavour to reach a consensus about already understood and shared objects, for the purpose of obtaining mutually or generally beneficial outcomes such as greater social security. It will commend and endorse some beliefs as true and caution against the truth of other beliefs. Likewise, dialogue 2 will employ a formal concept of truth. However, neither area of dialogue will claim to represent something called "truth".

Non-representational religious pluralists suggest that inter-religious dialogue allows people with different religious beliefs to understand each other and to reach agreements without requiring that they necessarily share all of each other's true beliefs. Inter-religious dialogue does not aim at getting anyone any closer to the "truth of the meaning of things". Consequently, they cease to articulate religious diversity and inter-religious dialogue in terms that make religious dogmatism and metaphysical scepticism plausible. Instead, they settle for understanding (the aim of dialogue 2) and mutual agreement (the aim of dialogue 1). These two areas of inter-religious dialogue provide all the inter-religious truth anyone can expect to talk about.

Conclusion

Realist theories of truth still find their defenders, but the non-representational theory of true beliefs outlined here should be congenial to the theological outlook of many members of the Sea of Faith Network. As well as articulating a different pluralistic account of inter-religious dialogue, it locates a religious response to life in a context that breaks free from both religious dogmatism and metaphysical scepticism. For non-representational religious pluralists, accepting that religious beliefs are of value no longer demands accepting ecclesiastical or philosophical dogmas about the nature of reality. Equally, rejecting particular religious beliefs, or even rejecting religion in general, no longer implies some form of metaphysical scepticism. Instead, the difference between those people who accept religious beliefs and those who reject them will amount to a historical disagreement about the usefulness of the purposes religious beliefs serve.

Perhaps the challenge for the Sea of Faith Network in the coming millennium is to show why religious beliefs continue to remain useful. Initially this may be a lonely and agonising endeavour. It may just also be the beginning of a new much needed religious reformation in which, among other things, truth will no longer be set alongside understanding and agreement as a goal of inter-religious dialogue.

UNDERSTANDING, INSPIRATION AND SUPPORT

Robert Ashby

How strange it would have seemed to me only a few years ago that I would now be thinking, speaking and writing so much about religion. I have always lacked that "God-shaped hole", and have no natural affinity with ceremonial or ritual. I was not christened; compulsory school chapel services are memorable for the wonderful smell of the chapel, good glass, and a few still haunting hymn tunes. I seem not to have needed another layer of explanation for my emotional responses to nature or human life.

Through working in a humanist organisation – a non-religious organisation! – I have to my surprise become immersed in matters religious. But this is with the protection of a diving suit: I look on objectively, fascinated but dry. It has been interesting to realise just how much religious history, theology, liturgy and culture I have absorbed in my non-religious life, beyond the ecclesiastical architecture that I had consciously studied. Religious echoes are all around us, secular nation that we are.

Encountering the Sea of Faith has been especially fascinating for me, perhaps because we share the clear starting point of religion as a human creation, or maybe because it has provided that rare opportunity to talk with people who are interested in the broad sweep of religion and civilisation, rather than one particular faith.

However, my encounters with Sea of Faith have also emphasised our differences. The conference I attended and the magazines that I have read together reinforce the distinction between Sea of Faith's *foundation* in religion and my *guided tour* of religion. For this reason, I have not joined the Network.

What is Sea of Faith for?
Friends of mine have struggled for years with their changing beliefs. Some who have been deeply religious find it perplexing that their faith ebbs and flows, rather than disappearing completely. But each person's path seems to lead gradually away from the superpurposive towards the humanistic. Where can he stop and rest on this meandering and stony path? He cannot write back to the home he left at the start, for he might then lose his welcome there before the path had revealed any future home at its end. And he cannot easily contact the several possible hous-

es that might lie ahead, for he does not yet know which might turn out to be a mirage, or which a hostile inn.

Thus the Sea of Faith is profoundly important. It comes into view just as the confused traveller is seeking a halfway house on that difficult journey. This, I think, is its most important role.

The halfway house

As an outsider to these friends' journeys, I cannot fully comprehend what they might need from a halfway house. But it is clear that a safe place and a safe listening ear are vital. These journeys also require stamina, tenacity and encouragement; there needs to be the opportunity to be with others on similar journeys, sharing experiences, and charting a mental map of where the path is leading and where it ends.

The Sea of Faith's annual conference has a warmth and humanity that most organisations would envy. This is excellent. The efforts to form regional groups and to hold meetings throughout the year are also good, especially at a time when local enterprise is increasingly met with indifference. The magazine is of high quality, but perhaps not entirely designed for the bedside tables of every lay halfway house. The challenge for Sea of Faith, if it seeks to develop a pastoral role, is to build additional and flexible mechanisms for "being there" throughout the year.

Where does the path lead?

One problem for Sea of Faith is that the path onward from its halfway house does not necessarily lead to a satisfactory new home. Some members may find themselves at one with the beliefs of the British Humanist Association, but at odds with our current lack of solutions to the need for fellowship and symbolic communal behaviour. For others it may seem that they are alone in their own unique theological position, but that they have no alternative to staying in their old home, with their minds floating or fighting elsewhere.

If Sea of Faith is to create a new home at the end of the path, there may be scope for development in such areas as liturgy, communal symbols, and some activity that suits a non-theistic worldview where religion still has importance as a human creation.

Such activity is inevitably bound into local structures and communities. While some fiery evangelists can achieve a little community and a lot of worship on the Internet, it would seem an impossible medium for framing new expression of complex beliefs, and handling existential anxiety. Face-to-face contact would seem to be essential.

Would the form of these activities be similar to those of Comte's followers, or would they be similar to those of BHA's own precursor, the Ethical Church, where Good replaced God, Shakespeare replaced Solomon, and Whitman replaced Wesley? Ironically, when I look at the Ethical Church's orders of service, dating from the very end of the nineteenth century, I can imagine them being successfully observed at a Sea of Faith conference today. That Church itself was a halfway house, and the existential questions of its congregation still exist in society today.

Another useful thread for Sea of Faith might be the development of an external focus, perhaps a traditional sense of charity, in order to provide another means of uniting members who might otherwise think they were divided by aspects of their changing beliefs. But this again requires inspirational and administrative input, in order not to reinvent the wheels on which so many churches run.

Radical belief?

Statistics continue to intrude into the field of religious belief, and the conflicting outcomes of polls and surveys unsurprisingly yield little of value. However, the figures can, with caution, be used to provide illustrations of trends.

If we combine figures for theistic belief, regular worship and perception of the basis of morality, it becomes clear that the theological basis of the Sea of Faith is not in itself so very radical these days – hence, perhaps, the resonance with the Ethical Church.

Most nominal Christians, for example, appear to see organised religion as entirely human in its development and (if they go on to consider the question) see the concept of religion itself as human in origin. They rarely pray with deep sincerity, yet probably believe collective worship in school assemblies is somehow a good thing, and are most likely to invoke God through the cultural reflexes of swearing. However, I am sure that most of these millions, if pressed, would not *explicitly* endorse Sea of Faith's stance.

Traditional religious expression continues to hold the cultural high ground of propriety, and the moral high ground of unquestionable goodness, despite the civil wars that occur within and the onslaughts from without. One particularly important point in Britain is that religious questions tend not to be discussed in any depth. Broadcasting is shallow, and bookshops cater more for children's bibles and chicken soup than for deeper theological study.

Purely for personal interest, I made a few very brief summaries of books that have questioned traditional Christian theology and practice, and tried them out on a few friends who are at least nominally Christian. I asked them in what decade they felt that each book had been published. The answers hovered consistently around the 1960s; in fact all of them had been written well before the Great War!

Anyone who has had a sustained encounter with the policies and syllabuses of Religious Education in England and Wales will have noticed a similar time warp; it is as though the past hundred years or more of theology had never existed. Does any RE syllabus say explicitly under "Creation Stories" that the Anglican Church accepts evolution, but with God at the helm? Sadly, one usually finds the old poles-apart presentation of scripture and science. In RE syllabuses, all Muslim men attend the mosque, Jews attend the synagogue, and Christians attend a church. RE is remote from religion today. In mainstream publishing, too, there seems to be a secret campaign to silence radical theology, apart from the occasional voice given to Freeman and Cupitt.

Although the Church of England and the moderate elements of most organised religions in Britain have changed enormously in the last century, they have done so without engaging the public, and so can easily pretend that their new veneers are old and solid oak. I claim that there is more substance in William James than in most contemporary "spiritual" guidance.

Philosophy is beginning to emerge from its shell and is working through the popular media to bring critical thinking and a rational basis for ethics to bigger audiences via new magazines, television programmes and illustrated books. Yet theology is still unable to communicate. Schools and religious broadcasts present a Christianity that is at odds with so much in present-day churches and individual Christians' minds. Perhaps Richard Holloway's *Godless Morality* has had such extraordinary success precisely because it brought the lay reader abruptly up-to-date: an Anglican bishop voicing what the millions of nominal Christians know to be practical, and sense to be true.

All this simply makes the job of the Sea of Faith more difficult, as it does the job of the British Humanist Association. It is difficult for either of us to appear radical when those who *should* be interested in one or both of our organisations have firstly not had access to the story of the paths we've travelled so far, and, secondly, have been told by implication that this story is really not worth bothering with.

The radical aspect of Sea of Faith is thus probably not its stated beliefs, but rather its members' processes of coherent questioning, and the shared desire that such questions be asked and resolved in each individual's life.

Radical action?

What does Sea of Faith need in order to have more influence and reach more people? It must first of all deal with the future, not try to alter the past. What are the long-term goals that Sea of Faith extrapolates from its basic tenets? If it could really change organised and personal religion, what changes would it seek? As is found among the freethinkers of Humanism, it can be understandably hard to pin down a consensus of aims, but the discussion is revealing, and can be made interesting to the outside world.

My experience of both BHA and Sea of Faith conferences reveals a shared paradox. While both organisations are concerned with moving away from the unquestioned status quo, the assembled members seem more concerned with the past. For example, BHA participants often talk with passionate antipathy towards the actions and beliefs of religions, while Sea of Faith participants rail against the structures and strictures of the churches. Few at either event speak with vision and passion about other futures: the destination home, and the roads to get there. Both organisations have the challenge of building more interest in the positive and visionary elements that are the proper reasons for our existence.

A second essential for Sea of Faith's growth and development is for it to consider if and how it can relate more closely to a wide range of people's daily lives, and how it can reach people where they live. The BHA also shares this need, and it is a big challenge. Indeed, our most radical action would be to achieve just that: to engage deeply and enduringly with the millions of non-believers and nominally religious people. It proves to be hard work, especially without resort to a team of spin-doctors, and in a situation where the media's fondness for soundbites can be more destructive than helpful.

The central purpose of our organisations needs to be framed in a way that genuinely engages a broad slice of the population, but without destroying the message and without being patronising. Words have to be backed up by the evidence of our organisational and individual lives: one cannot proclaim local relevance without providing the expected back-up and fellowship.

It is a strange mix of organisations that work in the existential sphere of being, finding meaning and purpose, and ultimately moving forwards. If, together, we were forced through the desperately difficult process of distilling our shared vision, I think the consensus would be simply that each and every human being should have access to the understanding, inspiration and support that are needed to live good and happy lives.

For the BHA, such *understanding* would include rationally derived knowledge as well as a moral understanding and an appreciation of the power of reason. *Inspiration* would include those elements that many might call "spiritual", and would also be a source of courage, happiness, and existential calm. But inspiration must also include the passion that can transform an understanding of humanist values into a moral commitment actually to live well, and transform the acceptance of humanist beliefs into a vast awe and sheer joy at the nature of being.

For a humanist organisation, the specific *support* needed by members is more difficult to pin down. BHA's work in conducting funerals is a clear area (demonstrated by a 50 per cent growth in 1999), as is a degree of fellowship and local activity. More imaginatively, support is also about the advancement of human rights and the values required by democracy, such as mutual tolerance and respect.

In essence, all the objectives that BHA derives from understanding, inspiration and support are framed by our search for the best in, and for, human life, and our aim to further humans' true nature and potential.

But what would be the objectives derived by the Sea of Faith?

At the most practical level of *understanding*, clear statements of Sea of Faith's approach to theology must be brought to congregations everywhere. A new introductory pamphlet could be publicised on small flyposters for church and meetinghouse notice boards. Sea of Faith should also have its Omega Course to complement that omnipresent Alpha. The compilations of members' personal beliefs and journeys are a magnificent resource and need to be on the religious shelves of each public library (purchased and donated by members of the Network).

What of the more difficult area of *inspiration*? Success here might rely on creating times and spaces in which members can safely speak of their personal and spiritual experiences and ideals. These opportunities thrive on good interpersonal contact, a sense of safety, a sense of being fellow travellers. Regional and local groupings of Sea of Faith should perhaps consider occasional days or retreats dedicated to creativity and inspiration, recharging members' sense of awe and wonder at the natural world and human life. These would need no recourse to jargon, to debates over the meaning of words such as "real", or to the soft euphemisms of "spirituality". The inspiration must spring from the emotions of every participant, avoiding the prison of language.

The *support* needed by Sea of Faith members will vary enormously, and much of it will not be openly admitted. Important too is how to support the many inquirers or potential members who have perhaps not yet reached that decisive moment of self-understanding and confidence. As well as the conferences, regional meetings and retreats, there must be some way of encouraging greater networking and informal contact. The local groups initiative could grow as a result, and the magazine grow likewise, with perhaps more personal content in addition to reviews and theology.

In conclusion

The Sea of Faith and the British Humanist Association share some practical challenges. We must get the general public interested in the questions we address, and be sufficiently attractive for our sympathisers actually to join. We must both pay even more attention to the business-like world of marketing and public relations, but we must balance this with the preservation of our values. Both organisations deal with complex and personal matters, and shallow marketing can lose as many old members as it gains new seekers.

But as I have suggested, we have dwelt too long on the theoretical, and re-living the battles of the past. None of that is radical today. We both need to stand back for a while and consider the future. What roles do we see for our organisations over the next twenty years, and how will we achieve the necessary changes?

Each of us has successfully followed small-scale strategies, which have led to organisational developments and good events, publications and publicity. But has either of us really engaged with the vastness of the issues we promote? Not yet. Is each organisation dominated by positive energy, pleasure and purpose? I don't think so.

Our organisations will both no doubt continue – with successes and failures, changes and consolidation. But if we do not achieve this greater engagement, this joy at our very existence, we will have avoided the colossal challenge that's there before us: almost welcomed, almost grasped.

UNREALITY

Pamela Donohue

There was a real God.
There was a real everything.
The world existed, without doubt.
Life was strong and good.
Living within ancient bounds
Of Book and age-old custom
Was granted, taken for granted

Then, one day, quite suddenly,
When no-one was looking,
Least of all myself,
Everything changed.
Nothing was ever the same again.
The Void was beckoning
And, faced with nothingness,
I moved to it to fling
My arms around its neck and cling
As fiercely as if it were a real thing.

BIBLIOGRAPHY

Bellah, Robert
 1970:   *Beyond Belief*, Harper and Row

Berlin, Isaiah
 1990:   *The Crooked Timber of Humanity*, John Murray
 1996:   "The Sense of Reality" in *Ideas and Their History*,
                 (Ed) Henry Hardy, Chatto and Windus

Borradori, Giovanna
 1994:   *The American Philosopher* (E.T. Rosanna Crocitto),
                 Chicago University Press

Bullock, Jude
 1996:   "Out in the Open Now, With Faith" in *Renew*,
                 September 1996

Cohn-Sherbok, Daniel
 1994:   *Modern Judaism*, Macmillan

Cupitt, Don
 1984:   *The Sea of Faith*, SCM Press
 1995:   *The Last Philosophy*, SCM Press
 1997:   *After God*, Weidenfeld & Nicolson
 1999:   *The New Religion of Life in Everyday Speech*,
                 SCM Press

Davidson, Donald
 1984:   *Inquiries into Truth and Interpretation*,
                 Clarendon Press
 1986:   "Empirical Content" in Ernest LePore (Ed), 1986,
                 op. cit.
 1990:   "The Structure and Content of Truth" in *The
                 Journal of Philosophy*, Vol. 87
 1994:   Donald Davidson in conversation with
                 Giovanna Borradori in Borradori, Giovanna,
                 1994, *op. cit.*
 1997:   "Gadamer and Plato's *Philebus*" in Hahn, Lewis
                 Edwin (Ed), 1997, *op. cit.*

Davies, Paul
1983: *God and the New Physics*, J. M. Dent (also published by Penguin 1990)

Eagleton, Terry
2000: *The Idea of Culture*, Blackwell

Eliot, T.S.
1948: *Notes Towards a Definition of Culture*, Faber & Faber

Elliott, Michael
1990: *Freedom, Justice and Christian Counter-Culture*, SCM Press

Freeman, Anthony
1993: *God in Us*, SCM Press

Freire, Paulo
1972: *Cultural Action for Freedom*, Penguin
1972: *Pedagogy of the Oppressed*, Penguin
1989: *Learning to Question: A Pedagogy of Liberation* (with Anthony Faundez), World Council of Churches

Gauchet, Marcel
1997: *The Disenchantment of the World*, Princeton University Press

Godwin, William
1926: *An Enquiry Concerning Political Justice*, Alfred Knopf

Goodman, Paul
1975: *Compulsory Miseducation*, Penguin

Hahn, Lewis Edwin (Ed)
1997: *The Philosophy of Hans Georg Gadamer*, Open Court
1999: *The Philosophy of Donald Davidson*, Open Court

Hick, John
1977:   *The Myth of God Incarnate*, SCM Press
1989:   *An Interpretation of Religion*, Macmillan Press

Hull, John
1985:   *What Prevents Christian Adults from Learning?*,
               SCM Press

Kaplan, Mordecai
1970:   "The Meaning of God for the Contemporary Jew"
               in A. Jospe (Ed) *Tradition and Contemporary Jewish
               Experience*, Schocken

Kuhn, Thomas
1970:   *The Structure of Scientific Revolutions*, Chicago
               University Press

Kung, Hans and Schmidt, Helmut (Eds)
1998:   *A Global Ethic and Global Responsibilities – Two
               Declarations*, SCM Press

LePore, Ernest (Ed)
1986:   *Truth and Interpretation: Perspectives on the
               Philosophy of Donald Davidson*, Blackwell

MacIntyre, Alasdair
1984:   *After Virtue: A Study in Moral Theory*, 2nd ed.,
               Notre Dame

Markham, Ian
1998:   "Truth and the Reality of God" in *Natural
               Theology*, T. & T. Clark

Miles, Jack
1997   "Religion Makes a Comeback", *New York Times*,
               December 7

Perry, Michael
2000:   *The Idea of Human Rights: Four Enquiries*, Oxford
               University Press

Robinson, John
1963:   *Honest to God*, SCM Press

Rorty, Richard
1980:   *Philosophy and the Mirror of Nature*, Blackwell
1989:   *Contingency, Irony and Solidarity*, Cambridge
                    University Press
1993:   "Human Rights, Rationality and Sentimentality" in
                    *On Human Rights: The Oxford Amnesty Lectures,
                    1993* (Eds) Shute, Stephen and Hurley, Susan,
                    Basic Books
1998   *Truth and Progress: Philosophical Papers Volume
                    Three*, Cambridge University Press
1999   *Philosophy and Social Hope,* Penguin

Samartha, S. J.
1991:   *One Christ – Many Religions: Toward a Revised
                    Christology*, Orbis

Shaw, Graham
1987:   *God in Our Hands*, SCM

Smith, Stevie
1983   "How Do You See?" in *A Selection* (Ed) Hermione
                    Lee, Faber & Faber

Smith, Wilfred Cantwell
1981:   *Towards a World Theology*, Macmillan Press

Society for Humanistic Judaism
1993:   *Guide to Humanistic Judaism*

Swidler, Leonard
1987:   "Inter-religious and Interideological Dialogue: The
                    Matrix for All Systematic Reflection Today" in
                    Swidler, Leonard (Ed) *Toward a Universal Theology
                    of Religion*, Orbis
1990:   "A Dialogue on Dialogue" in Swidler, Leonard (*et
                    al.*) *Death or Dialogue? From Monologue to the Age
                    of Dialogue*, SCM Press

Traer, Robert
1991:   *Faith in Human Rights*, Georgetown
                         University Press

Wiles, Maurice
1992:   *Christian Theology and Interreligious Dialogue*,
                         SCM Press

Williams, Raymond
1981:   *Culture*, Fontana

Willis, Paul
1990:   *Common Culture*, Oxford University Press

Wine, Sherwin
1985:   *Judaism Beyond God*, Society For Humanistic
                         Judaism
1988:   *Celebration*, Prometheus Books